JUANITA
The Life and Spirituality
of Saint Teresa of Jesus of the Andes

Jennifer Moorcroft

Copyright @2021 by Jennifer Moorcroft

All rights reserved. No part of this book may be reproduced in any form or by any electronic or mechanical means, including information storage and retrieval systems, without permission in writing from the publisher, except by reviewers, who may quote brief passages in a review.

This publication contains the opinions and ideas of its author. It is intended to provide helpful and informative material on the subjects addressed in the publication. The author and publisher specifically disclaim all responsibility for any liability, loss or risk, personal or otherwise, which is incurred as a consequence, directly or indirectly, of the use and application of any of the contents of this book.

WORKBOOK PRESS LLC
187 E Warm Springs Rd,
Suite B285, Las Vegas, NV 89119, USA

Website:	https://workbookpress.com/
Hotline:	1-888-818-4856
Email:	admin@workbookpress.com

Ordering Information:
Quantity sales. Special discounts are available on quantity purchases by corporations, associations, and others.
For details, contact the publisher at the address above.

ISBN-13:   978-1-956876-77-2 (Paperback Version)
            978-1-956876-78-9 (Digital Version)

REV. DATE: 08/12/2021

CONTENTS

Introduction   *i*

Chapter One
    Born in the midst of riches   1

Chapter Two
    My family, Those Beings I Love so Much   9

Chapter Three
    That Terrible Return to School   17

Chapter Four
    The Amazon   25

Chapter Five
    Mater Admirabilis   31

Chapter Six
    Dear Old Algorrobo   41

Chapter Seven
    Farewell To School   47

Chapter Eight
    I'm Famous For My Fits Of Laughter   51

Chapter Nine
    That Dovecote Nest   57

Chapter Ten
    The Horizons Are Infinite   65

Chapter Eleven
> **I'm Happy**   69

PART TWO
> **My Ideal, Jesus, My Infinite Ideal**   85

Chapter One
> **Caught In The Nets Of The Divine Fisherman**   91

Chapter Two
> **The Goal Of Prayer Is To Kindle In Us The Love Of Our God**   99

Chapter Three
> **Apostle Of The Eucharist Jesus Is My Nourishment**   113

Chapter Four
> **I Really Love The Most Holy Virgin**   127

Chapter Five
> **What Does Suffering Matter If A Person Loves?**   131

Chapter Six
> **This Darkness Is Followed By A Bit Of Light**   143

Chapter Seven
> **The Perfection Of Love**   155

PART THREE
> **Afterward Live In Love, Live In Heaven, Live In God**   163

The Legacy Of St Teresa Of Jesus Of Los Andes
> *I Wish I Could Set You Afire With That Love*   *173*

Bibliography   *197*

INTRODUCTION

21 March 1993, and before a massed crowd of thousands a huge banner unfurled down the facade of the Vatican, displaying the portrait of the Catholic Church's latest saint, Juanita Fernándes Solar, to be known officially as Saint Teresa of Jesus of Los Andes. She was the first native Chilean saint; she is the youngest Carmelite saint, only nineteen when she died, and the first Carmelite saint of the Americas.

Presiding over the ceremony, in his homily Pope John Paul II referred to the Gospel of the day, the incident of the man born blind and Jesus declaring Himself 'the Light of the World'; Juanita, too, he said, is given to us as a reflection of that light:

> God made shine forth in her in an admirable way the light of His Son Jesus Christ, so that she could be a beacon and guide to a world which seems to be blind to the splendour of the divine.[1]

It being the fourth Sunday of Lent, Laetare or 'Rejoice' Sunday, this was also appropriate for the new saint, of whom the Pope said:

> For her, God is infinite joy. This is the new hymn of Christian love that rises spontaneously from the soul of this young Chilean girl, in whose glorified face we can sense the grace of her transformation in Christ.[2]

The Pope saw in Juanita, St Teresa of Jesus of Los Andes, an inspiration especially for young people:

> She shouts it out particularly to the young people who hunger for the truth and seek a light which will give direction to their lives. To young people who are being allured by the continuous messages and stimuli of an erotic culture, a society which mistakes the hedonistic exploitation of another for genuine love, which is self-giving, this young virgin of the

Andes today proclaims the beauty and happiness that comes from a pure heart.³

St Teresa could be a guiding light for young people, he said, showing them the way to true, deep happiness, a very different path some young people had displayed during the Beatification Mass held six years earlier, 3 April 1987, in O'Higgins Park in Santiago, at which Pope John Paul 11 had also presided. Then, young people protesting against the Government, had let off smoke bombs. They were quickly ushered away, while the Pope, his eyes streaming, continued with the Mass. He was, after all, was no stranger to violent protest against the Church, having lived under both the Nazis and the Communists.

Saint Teresa of Jesus of Los Andes is a model not only for young people but for every Christian who longs to follow Christ more closely. She died young, but in the short span of her life she embodied, for Catholic and Orthodox Christians especially, in her sacramental life, the God-given means available to all, that would bring them to the goal of transforming union in Christ within the life of the Blessed Trinity. Living her baptismal promises to the full, strengthened by the Sacrament of Confirmation, fed almost daily on the Eucharist and finding increasing freedom from her faults through the Sacrament of Penance and Reconciliation, she came to live within the love of God that consumed her.

In this book, we will look at her life and the way she responded generously to God's call. She came to holiness within an ordinary life lived within her family, making friends at school, enjoying sports and horse riding during her holidays, exercising an apostolate during her holidays and among her fellow students at school. It was a holiness brought to the fullest fruition this side of heaven during her eleven months spent in Carmel.

Then in the second part, we will examine her inner life, the favoured ways in which God was guiding her. She may have been granted exceptional gifts to bring her to close union with God in a very short space of time, but the message contained within her life has relevance for us all. Quite simply, God wanted nothing less than everything from her, as he asks of all of us; we have Teresa's example, as she responded with great love and generosity in following his will.

In the third part we will follow the events after her death, the effect it had, firstly on her own family and her friends, then we shall see it spreading rapidly throughout Chile and beyond. We will summarise Teresa's message and its relevance for us all in living our Christian lives.

Each one of us has a unique calling from God, which he invites us to follow with a like love and generosity. We can call on the intercession of Saint Teresa of Los Andes, Juanita, that she will help us on our way.

At her canonisation, the Pope revealed the official name by which she would be called: Teresa of Jesus of Los Andes. This can be translated in English as Teresa of Jesus of the Andes. This title can expand her influence beyond the small town and monastery of Los Andes, but on consideration I have preferred to retain the original 'Los Andes'. Many saints are known by the place in which they were born, for example, St Teresa of Avila, or the place most associated with him, such as the Jean Vianney, the Curé of Ars. It emphasises either that they were born or lived in a particular place, but from there their influence is without boundaries because caught up in the limitlessness of God. Juanita Solar died in the little monastery of Los Andes, and this is now her proud title.

I wish to thank Fr Alexander of Mary Queen Beauty of Carmel of the Carmelite Fathers of Boars Hill, Oxford, England, for his encouragement in writing this book. It has arisen from a course I wrote for them on St Teresa of Los Andes, which is available on their website from February 2022, and Fr Alex was delighted that a book should accompany it. I hope that many people will be drawn to love this little Carmelite saint and be encouraged by her.

CHAPTER ONE
Born In The Midst Of Riches

Doña Lucia could hear the excited noise of the children playing in the spacious courtyard outside her window and looking out she could see the tousled head of her daughter, Juanita, almost lost in the crowd of children cheering on the runners in a race. She could see the determination on the face of her beloved daughter, near the front, determined to win, even against children older than herself and even against her boy cousins and her brothers. 'Don't think that Juanita was a little girl different from all the others', recalled Doña Lucia. 'She loved to play and was first in the games her brothers arranged. Sometimes I had to intervene to stop her since Juanita was too active in them, straining too much or playing at games that were more for boys. She usually won those games.'[4]

Nevertheless, her devout mother said a quick prayer that her daughter's strong will would be put, not at winning at any cost but used in the love of God in which she was bringing up all her children.

Juanita was a fighter, and as Ladisloa, the family coachman remarked, 'If this little girl came this far, it is a sign that the Lord wants her to do great things.'

Juanita Solar was born in Santiago on 13 July 1900. After a difficult birth, she was baptised two days later, and given the names Juana Enriquet Josephina de los Sagrados Corazones. Her name gives some insight into her family – she was named after her grandmothers, her mother had a devotion to St Joseph, hence her name Josephina and de los Sagrados Corazones because both her parents had a devotion to the Sacred Hearts of Jesus and Mary. She came from a deeply devout family and faith was the air she breathed from her birth.

Juanita lived with her parents, Miguel Fernandez Jarequamada and

Lucia Solar Armstrong, and her five brothers and sisters in the palatial mansion on Rosas Street, Santiago, owned by Lucia's father. Her mother was of Scottish descent, thus the name Armstrong. The wealthy Don Eulogio Solar was a doctor; he was also an astute businessman and owned estates and property all over the country. There were two other families living in the mansion, her aunt Juana, who was married to Doña Lucia's younger brother, Francis and their six children. There was also the Vicuña family with two children, so Juanita was surrounded by aunts and uncles, brothers, sisters and cousins. With so many children there was plenty of noise and laughter, as well as squabbles and fights. In the crowd of children Juanita, as she was always called, was a born leader. It was an idyllic childhood.

Her maternal grandfather was aristocratic as well as wealthy, so the families were in the upper rungs of Santiagan society. Juanita said that 'Jesus did not desire me to be poor like himself. I was born in the midst of riches, spoiled by all'. Despite her tomboy image, Juanita described herself as timid, gentle and sensitive. She was also energetic and enthusiastic for life.

At the age of six Juanita was sent to a school run by the Carmelite Sisters of Saint Teresa. She was there for only a month because of a misunderstanding. Her mother encouraged her daughter to tell her everything about her day, so in all innocence Juanita shared with her that one of the other little girls was not very nice, she was bullying her, pulling off her veil when they were in chapel. Her mother went to complain and Juanita described what happened then:

> As a result, the Mother Superior became angry. They put me in a room by myself on examination day and gave me bad marks. Then the Superior scolded me, saying that these things should not be told. I was surprised because I had always been told that I should tell my mother everything. They punished me. I cried a great deal, and when I got home my mother wrote a letter to the Superior telling her that I would not return to the school. I was happy because some of those little girls were very mischievous. There was one from whom I suffered because she was always trying to hurt me. When

we went to Chapel she always pulled my veil off. And I, being little, didn't know how to defend myself. I had a cousin whom they attacked often and I had to defend her. The others loved me.[5]

Juanita could not understand why she was being punished. She might have squabbles with her siblings and cousins, but they were not malicious, as some of the children were in the school. It must have been very difficult and bewildering for a little girl to be told that something she had always been told was right – telling her mother everything – was wrong. It is interesting that though she didn't defend herself, she could stand up for her cousin! And the Sisters were, of course wrong not to investigate the bullying.

There must have been something about Juanita that made her a butt of the other children's spite: they could see that in the chapel, even at that young age, Juanita was being drawn to prayer, so to having her veil pulled off was a distraction as well as an unhappy experience: did the little girl deliberately pull her veil off because she could see and perhaps was jealous of, Juanita's prayerfulness?

Her mother took Juanita out of the school, and later, when she was seven, she began school with the Sisters of the Sacred Heart on the Alamedawhich was known as the French School, because most of the Sisters were French-speaking. This was a very different experience, and Juanita thrived there, proving to be an excellent student.

All the children were taught to ride at an early age. Juanita described how her grandfather made her younger sister Rebecca and herself mount a horse each evening. He would toss a coin to see who would go first and, wrote Juanita, Rebecca always won. Don Eugenio was shrewd; he could see Juanita's competitive streak, and this was a lesson in how to come second gracefully – one hopes!

From the age of six, Juanita went every morning with her mother and her aunt Juana to Mass; this deepened the attraction she already had to prayer and she was deeply upset when she was told she was too young yet to receive Holy Communion, despite her many entreaties.

Then, when Juanita was seven, their beloved grandfather died with his rosary in his hand, while Mass was being said for him in an oratory at the side of his room. Juanita described how, 'prior to that, as the priest began to say Mass, Don Eulogio's face was filled with fear and he kept saying 'take him away', until Juanita's mother threw holy water at him and the satanic attack left him. 'His death', wrote Juanita, 'was that of a saint, as was his life.'

She would have been told those details later on, because the children were at Chacabuco at the time, perhaps because of his immanent death. They weren't told of their grandfather's death, but Luis, Juanita's younger brother, who was ill, suddenly shouted and cried out,' Why did they deceive me? Why didn't they tell me?' Later, Juanita saw her dead grandfather at the bottom of Rebecca's bed for eight days, which scared her so much she climbed into bed with her sister and the apparitions ceased. Juanita herself was overcome with grief at the death of her dearly loved grandfather and, as she said, cried an ocean of tears.

Don Eulogio's death meant an upheaval for all the families. They could no longer live in the mansion on Rosas Street, and his estates were divided up between the three families. Juanita's family moved to one of the houses they had in Santiago, a spacious mansion on Santo Domingo Street.

Juanita was confirmed at the age of nine with her brother Miguel and then began the preparation for making her First Holy Communion the following year. While the family had been on holiday at the holiday home in Chacabuco, her aunt Juana had given her niece a statue of the Virgin Mary, and from that time on, said Juanita, she had a great love for the Mother of God; with her help she began to overcome her faults. Always honest about herself, she said that she had a ferocious temper and irritability, while admitting that these fits of temper were far apart. Now, she said that no-one could make her lose her temper, although of course the other children tried their best. Her brothers deliberately tried to provoke her but without success. It was hard for her to bottle up her anger, though, for 'afterward, whatever displeased me made me cry and break into hysterical sobbing'.

A cousin said that he noticed a gradual change in her, as she became gentler and kinder, but Juanita noted in her diary the effort it sometimes took to overcome herself:

> It was costly for me to obey, especially when I was ordered to do something, then out of negligence I took my time in going to do it. Then I told myself that, even though they did not order me to do so, I would hasten to comply before the others. I didn't fight with the children. Sometimes I had to bite my lips and hurry to get dressed. I performed acts of virtue which I noted down in a little book. The book was full of my deeds.[6]

By June, the month of the Sacred Heart, her mother was so pleased with her daughter's progress in overcoming herself that she was happy for her to make her First Communion, 11th September. The day of her First Communion was unforgettable for Juanita: 'Oh, how my heart expanded!' she wrote in her diary later. 'For the first time I experienced a delicious peace'.[7] 'A delicious peace': preparing for this day had been a hard journey as she had tried to overcome herself, but this day she received the fruits of it. There was one little remark she also made that marked out the occasion as perhaps unusual: 'I experienced His dear voice for the first time'. She was already experiencing the voice of Our Lady. These were 'locutions' which she would receive throughout her life, both from Our Lord and Our Lady, guiding her and urging her on to greater self-giving.

Juanita thought that this happened to everyone and it was only a chance remark to her mother a while later that made her realise this was not so. Her mother was disturbed by what her daughter had told her and advised her to talk to the parish priest. Juanita, confused and embarrassed, was too ashamed to do so. It was only much later that she would speak of the exceptional graces she was receiving, and then only to her confessors and spiritual directors.

After making her First Holy Communion, all the family noticed the continuing change in her, as Luis testified: 'Daily contact with Our

Lord in Holy Communion transformed her. Juanita's temper became gentle and helpful. She was obedient and docile so that we, her brothers and sisters, noticed it, and she became an example to us.'[8]

The family moved to Ejerto Street shortly afterwards, and it was there that Juanita was guided by Jesus Himself into the path he willed for her. Every year she became sick on 8th December, the Feast of the Immaculate Conception, but it was on the third occasion, when she was fourteen, and had contracted appendicitis that the Lord's guidance became more specific. At that time appendicitis could be fatal, and Juanita described the events in great detail: the visits of her youngest brother, Ignacio; her friends, all in tears, convinced that, as she herself thought, she would die under the operation.

She didn't, she recovered, and she was sent to their hacienda in Chacabuco to convalesce. One day, when she was in bed, she was upset because her sister Lucia, who was also ill at the time and in another room, was getting more attention than she was, and she began to cry with envy. She then heard the voice of Our Lord, saying, 'What! I, Juanita, am alone on the altar for love of you and you can't even suffer one moment of solitude?' In this way 'He made me understand how abandoned and lonely He is in the tabernacle. He told me to keep Him company. Then He gave me my vocation, telling me that He wanted my heart to belong to Him alone, and that I should become a Carmelite. From that moment on I would spend the whole day in intimate conversation with Our Lord, and I felt happy alone.'[9]

This was a defining moment in her life. She was given to understand that her vocation was to be prayer and suffering for love of Our Lord. She also understood that she would become a Carmelite, although at that time she knew hardly anything about the Order.

Of course, Juanita didn't become a saint and happy to suffer overnight. She described an incident that happened not long after her serious illness. Her mother attributed her anger at the bathing pool to nervousness due to the anaesthetic, which wasn't fully developed in the early years of that century. Although the operation had been successful, Juanita developed serious postoperative complications because of the anaesthetic. This could explain why she behaved so childishly, still recovering from it, but Juanita was nothing if not honest about herself, not making excuses or blaming it on circumstances:

> For greater humiliation I will relate a fit of anger I had that was so great that it seemed to me that I was mad. The cause of it was that my sister and my cousin who was with us did not want to go bathing with us, because we were very small. It disgusted me that they called me 'little', so I didn't want to go swimming, but they forced me. When we were getting dressed the little girls came to hurry us up, but I answered them that I wouldn't get dressed until they left. They didn't want to leave, and my mother told me that I should dress. I, obstinately, didn't want to. My mother punished me but it was all useless. I began to cry and so great was my anger that I wanted to throw myself into the bathtub. My mamita began to dress me, but I kept on being angry. When I was ready, I repented of what I had done and I went to ask my mother's pardon.[10]

Her mother wasn't ready to forgive her so easily, which made Juanita even more inconsolable. Here, we see her strong will and also how, once she came to her senses, she could see how unacceptable her behaviour was, and was ready to seek forgiveness. (Her mamita, Ofelia Miranda, was a much-loved servant, very religious and good, who had looked after Juanita from her birth.)

CHAPTER TWO

My Family, Those Beings I Love So Much

The evening before she went to Confession for the first time, in an act that deeply moved the whole family, Juanita went round to them all, including their servants, begging their forgiveness for any hurt she had caused. Going first to her beloved, gentle father, he took her in his arms and with tears in his eyes assured his dearly loved daughter that she had never given him any reason to be displeased with her. Her mother, too, had tears in her eyes for this daughter who had grown so beautifully in the years during which she had tried to make herself more worthy to receive Our Lord for the first time.

It was in this warm, loving and Christian family that Juanita was happiest. Sixteen years separated her eldest sister, Lucia, from her youngest brother, Ignatio, so it was understandable that she was closest to her brother Luis, two years older, and the bubbly, happy-go-lucky Rebecca, two years younger than herself.

Her family, though, wasn't shielded from being tested with all the temptations and stresses of our own modern life. Loving her family so deeply, Juanita was distressed and troubled by all that her family went through. With her husband often away managing their estates, the running of the household fell in great part to their mother, and it wasn't easy for her to deal with all the problems that arose.

There was Miguel, for instance. He was five years older than Juanita, and was drifting in and out of the household, preferring to lead a somewhat bohemian and unconventional way of life, much to his mother's anger and distress. He was a gifted young man who loved poetry but he also loved alcohol, driving his mother to distraction in how to deal with him. He was profoundly religious, something that never left him, which endeared him to his younger sister. Juanita was increasingly finding herself in the role of peacemaker as she tried to encourage her mother to use kindness, the carrot, rather than the stick of her anger, but little success. Miguel said that only Juanita understood him, adding sadly: 'I don't fit in very well at home, but as for her, she's a real saint.'

Her mother was also being driven to distraction with her husband. Don Miguel was described as 'a morally good and upright man, never guilty of any offenses or scandals', but he had little education to help him in running their estates. To his wife's bitterness and anger, a bad harvest, a serious business misjudgement, and general mismanagement of their estates saw Lucia's legacy slipping away, and the family brought into, if not real poverty, a severe reduction in their wealth.

Juanita loved her father, but she was deeply hurt when she saw him drifting away from going to Mass. There was some excuse, because his work, supervising his properties, meant that he was often away from home for several months at a time, unable to attend Mass because of the lack of priests in so many parts of the country; it was easy to get out of the habit.

He was also someone who found it difficult to face up to awkward or difficult situations – he found it too hard to be there with the rest of the family when Juanita had her serious operation, for example - and it was easier for him to be away on business, rather than being at the sharp end of his wife's anger and disappointment with him when at home.

Juanita's letters to her father show the depth of her love for him, but her sadness, too, at not having her father with them, as well as describing all their activities while on holiday. She concluded one such description in a way that must have soothed the soul of her father as he saw his best efforts to manage their estates slipping away from him:

> As you can see, Daddy dear, the only thing lacking for our happiness is having you here. But while we're enjoying ourselves you're working, bearing the heat of the sun, providing for us.

Daddy, we don't know how to repay you for your great sacrifices. But your children recognize them and want to wrap you in our love and care. I think that is the best way to repay a parent. Why don't you try to get here, even if it's just for a few days? You don't know how bad I feel when I see the other girls so happy with their fathers. Come, please, because we have the joy of being so seldom with you during the year. The other day I was speaking with Don Julio Hurtado, and he spoke of you at great length.

Greetings and hugs from Mom and my brothers and sisters, and a great big hug from your daughter who loves you so much and who's always thinking of you. A great big hug, Daddy dear.

Juana, even though you don't send her greetings in your letter; but I'm over my anger about it anyway.[11]

Doña Lucia could be fastidious and demanding, with a quick tongue, but there was a deep bond between Juanita and her mother. She was perhaps the only one who understood her daughter's vocation to Carmel, and she also had a great respect for her. Deeply devout herself, she could discern in her daughter a genuine hunger for God.

Juanita's brother, Luis, later wrote a moving *Testimony* about his much-loved sister, which gives details about her that we would otherwise not know about. His room was next to hers, and sometimes in the early morning he could hear her singing softly in her beautiful contralto voice and playing on a small organ, left to her by her grandfather. 'I like to greet the Lord singing', she said in explanation.

Going past her room, he would quietly open her door and was often able to see her so absorbed in prayer that she was oblivious to his presence. In a lovely phrase, Luis said that 'Her soul was ever on its knees before God' and said how totally immersed in God she could be when at prayer:

Every time I saw her alone in her room, when I opened her door,

I would find Juanita immersed in deep prayer. She seemed capable of superhuman concentration, so much so that I didn't dare speak to her until she realized I was there. In church she adored the Lord on her knees, totally unaware of anything that was occurring.[12]

It was Luis who gave a her a rosary and taught her how to pray it. They made a pact together to say it every day. Juanita said there was only one time when she forgot to say it.

From the time the family had lived with their grandfather, Juanita would have noticed how generous all her extended families were to the poor. It stemmed from Don Eugenio, who made sure his workers were well looked after, materially and spiritually, and no poor person knocking on their door was sent away empty. Juanita had the same concern for the poor. Luis gave this testimony:

> Juanita's charity was without limit toward the poor people who visited our home. I saw her waiting on them with her own hands hundreds of times, taking them food and clothing with a loving smile.
>
> Juanita would take medicine to the tenant farmers on our lands or to some sick person in a peasant household. Juanita also cared for these people with her own hands. Sometimes she broke away from the family quarters and went up to the third patio where the employees lived. There she would invent ways to help them with so much naturalness and grace that the employees didn't notice.[13]

She personally took a young, neglected orphan boy, Juanito, under her wing. She saved the pesos her mother gave her as pocket money and gave them to Juanito. She couldn't hide from her mother what she was doing, who responded with a smile, and exclaimed, 'Juanita and her ways!' She taught him the catechism and how to pray, giving him food, buying socks and underwear for him with her own pocket money. To Luis, she said he was a symbol to her of all the poor neglected children in the world. She couldn't help everyone, but she could help one of them.

In assessing Juanita's character, the testimony that Luis wrote about his sister is invaluable because it enables us to see Juanita from the outside, as it were, by one who was very close to her. He left some impressions of his sister as a young child as she began to co-operate with God in overcoming her faults:

> Juanita was a very emotional person; she used to blush when something bothered her, but she controlled herself. She didn't let herself get carried away by her temperament and feelings. On the contrary, when I offended her, Juanita's first impulse was to pay me right back in the same way, but she used to get hold of herself and say to me, 'I won't do anything to you'. Her self-control was most evident when someone annoyed her during a game. From the time she was a little girl, Juanita often deprived herself of eating things she really liked.[14]

Then, Luis described her as she stepped out into young womanhood:

> Juanita was very attractive physically, her way of expression was very pleasant and agreeable. She was quite tall, well shaped, had a certain majesty of movement, white skin and blue eyes. Her head was small and her hair was light brown. She had a really pleasing voice. You could recognise great strength in her deep gaze. She was a very quiet person, very much in control of herself. Juanita could hide her emotions; that's why I never saw her cry. Juanita was joyful and always seemed happy. Her joy was neither loud nor boisterous.[15]

> I remember my sister as always being in control of herself. I don't remember witnessing any temper tantrums. Her character

was tranquil and calm. Her will was energetic and ironlike, without seeming so. She had a sense of humour. Juanita's natural way was to go along unnoticed. She was happy and easy to get along with because she was very noble in her way. She liked to be rather quiet and only spoke up when asked a question. One noticed that she had something going on inside which made her seem introverted. I was aware that she was taken up with the idea of God's presence.[16]

As for Juanita herself, on her fifteenth birthday she felt she was on the brink of a very special year in her life, writing in her diary, alluding to a vow of virginity she had recently made:

> Fifteen is the most dangerous age for a young girl because it marks her entrance into the tempestuous sea of the world. But now that I'm fifteen years old, Jesus has taken command of my ship and has protected it from encountering other vessels. He has kept me in solitude with Himself. Consequently, my heart, by knowing this Captain, has fallen under the spell of His love, and here He keeps me captive. Oh, how I love this prison, and this powerful King who keeps me captive, and how I love this Captain who amid the waves of the ocean doesn't allow me to suffer shipwreck.[17]

Unsurprisingly, Juanita became more and more a stabilizing influence within her family, who appreciated her calming influence when many problems arose.

Juanita, meanwhile, was beginning to waken to the vocation to Carmel God had given her. She knew almost nothing about Carmel, so began to read the autobiography of St Thérèse of Lisieux, a young French Carmelite who had died at the age of twenty-four in 1897. It is customary for a Carmel to send round to other Carmels an account of the deceased sister's life. The Lisieux Carmel compiled some writings of Thérèse under the title of *Histoire d'une Ame*. It was soon circulating far beyond the monastery walls and taking the world by storm as people in all walks of life were captivated by her *Little Way* of complete trust in the good God. Likewise, the *Souvenirs* of Elizabeth of the Trinity were circulating, another Carmelite, who had died at the age of twenty-six in the Dijon Carmel in 1906, so she was a close contemporary of Juanita herself.

These were the first writings about Carmel that Juanita absorbed as she began to understand the life and spirituality of the Order. It was unlikely that they had been translated in Spanish at the time, so Juanita, who spoke French fluently, would have read them in the original. It was Elizabeth's spirituality that began to attract her most and which more nearly corresponded to her own.

As she approached her fifteenth birthday, she was taking her Carmelite vocation seriously. Juanita had expected her birthday to usher in a new departure for her, but she was totally unprepared for the bombshell her mother dropped, which only later did she see as God's plan in preparing her for Carmel.

CHAPTER THREE

That Terrible Return To School

Juanita loved to be at home, surrounded by family, with aunts, uncles and cousins nearby, so it was a severe shock when, as she turned fifteen, her mother told her that she and Rebecca would be returning to school as boarders.

Until now, Juanita and Rebecca had been attending the elementary school of the Sacred Heart on the Alameda, which was near the family home on Ejercito Street. When the family moved again, to 92 Vergara Street, to continue there, the two girls would have to pass the Jesuit High School for Boys, whose students liked to admire the girls as they walked by. Pretty Rebecca and the beautiful Juanita, with her statuesque figure and gracefulness, would certainly have attracted their interest. To avoid this, Doña Lucia decided that they should go immediately to the other Sacred Heart school, the High School college on Maestranza Street, known as the English School, because most of the Sisters were English-speaking, rather than waiting to graduate from the elementary school first. It was too far away from their new home to go as day girls; they had to become boarders.

The Order of the Religious of the Sacred Heart was founded by St Sophie Barat and had an excellent reputation for the high standard and range of their studies. Their aim was to give to their students a good grounding in their faith, along with their other studies, so that when they left school they would be well prepared for life in the world and with a sound grasp of their faith, which could withstand the obstacles to belief and the worldliness they would meet with later in life. It is to their credit that many of the girls they taught entered the Order to become nuns and teachers themselves.

As well as the usual school subjects, Juanita now also studied philosophy, logic, ontology and psychology. Her favourite subject was, of course, religious studies, but she also excelled in history and literature. All this training is reflected in her letters, where she expresses herself with clarity, honesty and graciousness. She valued the education she was being given, writing in her diary, 'the education of women is even more important than that of men, for the women will educate the man'.

Luis described his sister's training in theology at her school, which gave her such a good grounding in understanding her faith and the ability to pass it on to others:

> She easily learned the classic physical proof arguments for the existence of God. Even the most difficult concepts such as potency and act, causality and contingency were easy for her. I remember that she would become impatient if someone interrupted our conversations. She always wanted to talk about the person of Christ rather than about theoretical subjects. She preferred to see God incarnate and acting in the sacred person of Christ. Juanita was in love with Christ.
>
> She possessed a keen mental solidity and continual thirst to investigate and know. Perhaps this aided her in her mystical, bold and deep insights.[18]

Unfortunately, the same excellent education Luis was being given at his Jesuit school on Maestranza Street had the opposite effect on him. While studying philosophy, to Juanita's great sorrow, he began to doubt his faith and moved away from God, or as he put it, 'I was forgetting about God'. The world, which to Juanita showed forth the grandeur and love of God, was to him a barren nothingness, and nothing his sister said would persuade him otherwise.

At first Juanita hated being a boarder; she called the school a prison, with all its rules and regulations, after the freedom she had at home. In letters to her friends she said she wished it would burn down; as summer holidays drew to a close she said the thought of returning to it gave her goosebumps, which was probably schoolgirl hyperbole, but nevertheless it was a distinct contrast from family life. It was strict, it had rules which the girls, of course, would try to circumvent. Because the nuns had the right to read their letters the girls overcame that obstacle by keeping a notebook in which they would write to each other; they would then circulate it among themselves without the nuns knowing about it -although they probably did!

In a letter to her friend Carmen Ortúarz she suggested she write her letters to her in a code the girls used at school, representing vowels with Roman numerals, 'if by chance they're [the nuns] are pillaging through my letters'. It was little wonder that Juanita found it so much more restricting after the freedom of their holidays and the warmth of her family home. She found it very hard to adapt to boarding school life as her friend Elena Gonzales said:

> She had a lot of trouble in adolescence when her parents took her out of the day school and registered her at the boarding school, she was not pleased with the decision because she loved her family very much and wanted to be with them. God, who knows how to do things, permitted separation from the family in order to prepare her for the definitive separation of the Carmelite cloister. She resigned herself, and she overcame her personal displeasure through strength of will. She entered the boarding school with a determined spirit, and her displeasure was not even noticed.[19]

Her first months at boarding school were not helped by little Ignacio hurting his leg badly and having to go to hospital. His mother went to be with him, which left Juanita grieving, not only for her beloved little brother and that she couldn't be with him, but also that her mother wouldn't be coming for her usual visit to see them at the weekend.

Knowing the sacrifices her parents were making to send all of their children to good schools, Juanita was determined not to let them down and to do her studies to the best of her ability. She had an additional, even more important motive. In a letter to her friend Graciela Larraín, who also hoped to become a Carmelite, she describes how she approached her studies and what the school expected of them, all in the context of 'just as Jesus would have done'. They were living under a rule at present, school rules, just as, later on, they would be living under the Carmelite Rule, she said:

> We must say the same thing at every moment of our lives, and do it through the exact fulfilment of our duties. Even though no-one sees us, let's keep the school rules, which is the rule that we have right now; for example, in our classes by applying ourselves to our studies, even when we don't want to, just as Jesus would have done. Through poverty by not wasting anything and not spending anything on ourselves, but always being mindful of the poor. Through chastity, by being as pure as the Virgin and not allowing any love to concern us but the love of God, so that we don't fail in our duties. We'll know the intensity of His love through the love we have for our neighbour.[20]

Already, with her heart set on Carmel, she now saw the boarding school as the first step in detaching herself from those she loved in preparation for her entry into Carmel: 'Despite my pain, the least I could do was to thank the Lord,' she wrote in her diary, who was paving the way so I would become more apart from the things of the world. He was calling me to be with Him, so I'd become accustomed to live more apart from my family before my entrance into Carmel'.[21]

Aware that her parents were making great sacrifices to send her to such a good school, because they realised the value of a good education, Juanita set about to doing and being the best she could for them. There is a later incident that shows Juanita's wisdom and maturity and her understanding of the situation. At school she excelled at her studies and her confessor, knowing her desire to enter Carmel and to test her, asked her if she had the humility to fail her exams. This was a big ask, but Juanita's answer was, No, but not from pride at her achievements. She gave her reasons: she wanted to please her parents who were making sacrifices to give her a good education. She didn't want to fail her exams and give the impression that, simply because she was going to enter Carmel, her grades didn't matter. And she wanted to use the gifts God had given her to the best of her ability.

Much later, she had a conversation with Luis and gave another reason. He couldn't understand why she, who was gifted with so many talents and abilities, should throw it all away to enter an enclosed Order. Juanita replied that, yes, she did have gifts, 'but how can I give greater glory to God than by giving myself over entirely to him and using my faculties, both intellectual and moral, day and night, to know and love him?' She didn't want to give God second best.

Juanita and Rebecca started as boarders in July, and in September she had what she called a 'decisive interview' with Mother Rios, her spiritual director. Mother Rios had been at the elementary school when Juanita first started there, and after an illness transferred to Maestranza Street. Juanita was delighted to know this holy Sister once again, who had already discerned in the young girl the stirrings of a vocation. The interview was decisive, because it was probably the first time she had spoken to anyone about it, and speaking out loud at last gave it substance. From then on the nun would be a wise and understanding guide for her. The first step was that Mother Rios said that Juanita should begin a diary of her spiritual journey, a diary which now gives us an unsurpassed mirror into Juanita's soul.

It was to be a diary not merely recounting external events, Juanita realised, as began writing, dedicating it to Mother Rios with these words:

> Dear Mother: You believe you are going to find an interesting story, but I don't want you to be deceived; the story you are going to read is not the story of my life, but the intimate life of a poor soul who, without any merit on her part, Jesus Christ loved in a special way and filled abundantly with His favours and graces.[22]

By this time Juanita had been going to a few parties and dances organised in their home, and an admirer had even come round with a bunch of flowers for her. Mother Ríos said that if she was serious about her vocation then she had to be wary of going further than the *polelo,* a friendship that had not gone so far as 'going steady'.

She also warned Juanita of the austerity of the Carmelite life, knowing that, despite her ability at sports, her health was delicate: 'Do you have the necessary health? Do you feel strong enough for this vocation?' This was a constant worry for Juanita herself, and something that would be of great concern to her throughout her school days.

Mother Izquierdo, the sister in charge of the students, also had a great influence on her, but perhaps because of Juanita's frail health thought that she didn't have a vocation to Carmel. When she had a bad tooth and a headache, Mother Izquierdo came to her room and gave her advice that, said Juanita, Our Lord had also given her in other trying circumstances: 'My child, Jesus loves you very much. He surrounds you with His Cross. Offer this pain like a flower for your Communion tomorrow'. 'I love this sister very much', commented, Juanita. 'She's a true saint.'

Juanita made a wide circle of friends at school. All her friends were unanimous is saying she was a terrific friend to have, discreet and trustworthy. She had a happy temperament, always even-tempered, although reading her diary and knowing the struggles and the pain of her ill-health that she was normally able to conceal, this was exceptional in itself. She was kind to the other children, giving a discreet helping hand and encouragement when necessary. She was popular and a born leader. There is a very simple example of the influence she had on others: the girls were meeting with Mother Ríos one day and with her head so full of Carmel, Juanita sat on the floor as she thought she would be doing in Carmel. The other girls, not knowing her motives, followed her example and sat on the floor, too.

Life in the boarding school was not all study and gloom for her. They had a free day in September for Mother Izquierdo's feastday. The girls played a game of hide and seek and a game of catch the flags. Juanita's side won 'and we were very happy'. She came first in a handwriting competition and a few days later she went with a group of friends for a walk along the Alameda, where they bumped into Miguel who was doing his military service. Juanita was pleased to learn that he had been promoted to corporal, the head of his squad.

She became a boarder, then, with distaste but with a determination to do her best and not let God and her parents down. Fortunately, since the girls had started school in the middle of term they were soon on their way for the usual family holiday.

CHAPTER FOUR

The Amazon

Every year the extended family spent their Spring and Summer holidays in the country, on their farms and estates or with friends. Their favourite holiday home was the beautiful and luxurious hacienda at Chacabulco in the north of the country, with its 23,000 acres of land. After their grandfather's death it passed to their uncle Francisco Solar and his family.

Arriving there on the 16th September, Juanita luxuriated in the freedom and enjoyment that lay ahead for her: 'I find myself in the country. We arrived at 5 o'clock. We walked all over. What happiness!'

There were long days for the young people to enjoy themselves, horse riding, playing tennis, swimming, flying kites, exploring the beautiful countryside. For Juanita it spelt freedom and the enjoyment of being with her family, relations and friends. Horse-riding was a great love, and she was a superb horsewoman, so much so that she was nicknamed the Amazon. When they discovered tennis, Juanita was a strong and determined player. As she wrote to her friend Herminia Ossa:

> Have you gone horseback riding very much? As for me, I'm making up for last year. We've had some great outings here with Tere Jara, my cousin, who is here. We have a good time with her. The other day we went to have lunch in the hills, leaving at 6 in the morning and riding all day long. We arrived near the mountain range, which is pretty far away and after lunch we went horseback riding again and didn't get home till eight o'clock. We travelled fifteen leagues.

What do you think of that? But these happy days will turn into those sad school days and that will soon be here. I get discouraged when I think of it.

On nights when the moon is out we go out as soon as we finish our meal and go to the haystack where we spend our time singing. During the day we play croquet. We have a lovely playground. I must tell you that I have become quite a seamstress, too, something rare for me, who, as you know, am so lazy.[23]

With the help of the Heart of Mary priests, the family always organized a Mission for the local people and estate workers when they were on holiday. Juanita enjoyed, especially, teaching the children their catechism and organizing games for them. She was so good with children that a friend was convinced she would join an active teaching Order such as the Sacred Heart sisters.

What she described to her friend Carmen during their November – March holidays 1916, giving the statistics for the mission, was typical of these missions.

They preached very well, and everybody was pleased. Each day we taught catechism to the children, 24 of whom made their First Communion; 619 people received Communion; 70 were confirmed and there was one wedding. What do you think of that? On Sunday, the last day of the Mission, we had a procession of the Most Blessed Sacrament. The farm hands had formed circles everywhere the Blessed Sacrament was to go. There were three altars, two of which the men decorated themselves, the other arranged by us.[24]

Her friend Maria Ramirez testified to the love and enthusiasm with which Juanita threw herself into teaching catechism to the children:

Juanita distinguished herself in the way she taught catechism and prepared the poor children and the children of the tenants for their First Holy Communion, teaching them the truths of their religion. She did this during the vacation period at the Chacabulco Hacienda and at other family estates. Instead of taking a break during vacations, Juanita sacrificed herself out of love of God and to help them come to a knowledge of the faith.[25]

Soon, though, it was time to return to school, 'only seven days before we must be in that dungeon. My blood runs cold, just thinking about it', she added in her letter to Carmen.

On her return to school, Juanita made another decision about her journey to Carmel. She had accepted that being at boarding school was preparing her for the separation of Carmel. Now she shared 'the secret of my life' with Rebecca on her fourteenth birthday, considering that her younger sister was old enough to understand what she was going to tell her. 'Believe me, Rebecca, at 14 or 15 one understands one's vocation. You hear a voice and a light shows you the path of your life':

> That beacon shone for me when I was 14 years old. I changed my course and planned the path that I had to follow, and today I come to share with you my secrets and the ideal projects I have forged ... Very soon we'll be taken from one another, and the desire we have always cherished in our childhood of always living together will quickly be shattered by another higher ideal of our youth ... I've been captured in the loving nets of the Divine Fisherman...
>
> On the 8th December I promised myself to Him. It's impossible to say how much I love Him. My mind is filled with Him alone. He is my ideal, my infinite ideal. I long for the day when I can go to Carmel to devote myself to Him alone, to abase myself before Him and so live His life alone: to love and suffer that I may save souls.[26]

Juanita

It was unlikely that her beloved younger sister, so different in character from Juanita, really understood or took in what her sister was telling her. She herself had no intention in becoming a nun: she was looking forward to parties and dances. But for Juanita the step had been taken and she would not look back.

The family returned to Chacabulco for their holidays as usual, at the beginning of 1917. Juanita noted in her diary on New Year's Day, 'One year closer to my homeland'. They found there was a great build-up in the area due to the war in Europe. South American countries tried to be neutral but they had to be prepared. It seemed that they visited a museum or two, and Juanita adds an intriguing detail of a poetic captain, as she wrote to Carmen Ortuzar:

> We're all getting along very well, and we live a rather tranquil life, which is what I love most. Remember that on February 12, there are military manoeuvres. Many people will be coming and there's a regiment patrolling the roads here, and the regimental captain is very entertaining. He recites verses of poetry and sings.
>
> We haven't gone on any great outings, because the younger children are off to the mountains for six days. I assure you that I envy them with my whole soul. I want you to know that I'm completely versed on the Battle of Chacabuco. The captain taught us about it at the battle ground.
>
> The interesting thing about Chacabuco is the excavations that have been made at the Indian cemetery where they've discovered beautifully painted pieces of pots and plates. Even though they've been buried for a century, they are perfectly preserved, and one can see the progress they made, as there are some – the most primitive ones – that are made of mud. Others are of baked clay and painted in different colours. They've also discovered bullets and other pieces of artillery; the latter are quite large and heavy. And to think they're only pebbles compared with those used in warfare today.[27]

It was a quieter holiday, she said, with fewer rides and excursions in the countryside, perhaps because of the military build-up, adding in her letter to Carmen:

> I haven't much to tell you, for we haven't gone horseback riding more than 10 times since we've been here. How does that strike you? We used to go out in the evening and in the morning. In the afternoons we used to go for a walk, and we almost always went to the Hermitage of the Most Blessed Virgin up on a mountain. That's where I pray and interceded for you...
>
> We spend our days reading and knitting under the trees. We read 'The Account of a Sister' [a rather sentimental novel] together, and I'm reading it a second time because I'm fascinated with it; and, of course, I'm praying. You can't imagine how short the days are, and how quickly they pass, now that I'm beginning to think of the terrible return to school on the 8th.[28]

Juanita was, of course, praying and she began reading the *Life* of St Teresa of Avila; in February the family joined a pilgrimage to the Chilean Lourdes replica, writing after what was a very moving occasion for her:' Yes, Mother, you are the celestial Madonna who guides us. You allow heavenly rays to fall from your maternal hands. I didn't believe such happiness could exist on earth; yesterday my heart was ecstatic at your virginal feet.'[29]

When she had a letter from Mother Ríos while on holiday, with her delicacy in preserving herself totally for Our Lord, she worried if she were not loving the nun too much. It is also an insight into the small unseen sacrifices Juanita made while at school:

> Today I heard from Mother Ríos. She sent us her greetings. I so love that sister that I must overcome myself so I'll not love her too much and write to her. If she knew the sacrifices I made so I would not have to take time out from my studies. But, in the

end, God knows these sacrifices and the fact that I offered them for her intentions so that He'd grant them.[30]

CHAPTER FIVE
Mater Admirabilis

The new term at school brought joys and trials for Juanita. True to her resolve to do her very best in her studies, she thought she was stupid and was totally unaware of her beauty, her intelligence and her attractiveness. She was surprised and delighted, then, when she came top in History, her first success. She immediately attributed her success, not to herself but to Jesus through Our Lady:

> June 27. I came out first in my history class. I'm happy. Never before did I have positions of honour, and now the Virgin is giving them to me. I also asked for them to please my father and mother and, above all, because this is my last year at school and I want to leave a good impression so people see that, even though I'm thinking of becoming a Carmelite nun, I did apply myself to my studies. I find that I'm stupid and if I'm granted positions of honour they are due to Jesus and my Mother. I love her. She is so good![31]

It was only the first of such awards, because she usually came top of her class in most subjects The one subject she didn't like was chemistry, but she studied extra hard, coming top of the class in that, too.

Aware of the influence she had with the children, she wanted to use it for good, noting in her diary a couple of occasions when she 'exercised her apostolate':

> Today I exercised my apostolate. I gave good advice. Jesus inspired me with it. I also made three young girls take their soup,

encouraging them to perform little deeds for the good Jesus. Furthermore, we went to see a little sick girl. So, we had the chance to perform an act of charity. Jesus, my dear, when will I be at your side? I love you! I desire to unite myself to You eternally.[32]

A little girl whom they had severely upbraided and threatened to take away her sash was so filled with despair that she was going to persuade Mother Izquierdo to take her sash away from her. I prayed a *Memorare* to the Most Holy Virgin, and I told the little girl all that Mary inspired me to say in order to encourage and console her. I spoke to her of the Virgin, that she should tell Mary all her troubles and ask her protection; that if she suffered with patience, she would have a great reward in heaven.[33]

In June, on the Feast of the Sacred Heart, Juanita had the great joy of receiving the coveted medal as a Child of Mary, given to the best students and those who gave the best example. She took the honour very seriously, nearly always signing her letters H.M. from the Spanish. Referring to her vow of virginity, she wrote in her diary:

Not only am I the spouse of Jesus, but today I have united myself even more to Him. I am His sister. I am the child of Mary. From today on, like the princesses brought to the palace of the betrothed to be formed like Him I now also am going to enter into my soul, the house of God. There my Mother and my Jesus await me. Oh, how I love Him![34]

Also in June, in another major step in her journey to Carmel, Juanita wrote a letter to her friend Graciela Montes, nicknamed Chela, (Letter 12), revealing her vocation. With Graciela having a sister, Mother Teresa, in the Los Andes Carmel, it was a good way for her to find out about Carmel. She asked her friend for a copy of the Carmelite Rule, and Graciela showed her a letter she had received from her sister.

'What a wonderful letter!', Juanita shared with her. 'I'm happy to have read it. This is the first time I received anything from a Carmelite. What a delightful beginning'.

Visiting Mother Teresa, Graciela showed her some of those notebooks that the girls passed round, in which Juanita had written something; Mother Teresa remembered that she had held Juanita in her arms as a baby. Mother Angelica, the Prioress, reading them, too, sent Juanita a medal and, sensing from what Juanita had written, that she might have a Carmelite vocation said she should write to her.

Juanita's joys swiftly turned into other trials. Misunderstandings arise, even in a convent. One of the nuns had given bad example, Juanita said something about it, and this unleashed a storm over her head. Juanita had such a high regard for the religious state that seeing a sister fail made her doubt her own vocation. Because of her stand she was misjudged, but she gave it all to God and prayed for those who had misjudged her. As she wrote about the incident in her diary she ended by realising that only God can judge our motives, which in her case Juanita felt had been justified; He is the only One to whom we need turn our eyes:

> June 25. I have known one thing and I'm at the point that I can suffer no more pain. It would have been better not to know anything. My God, I offer that to You. I know You are my protection. I beseech You for that person.
>
> June 26. I felt distressed. I hardly dare look at Mother Izquierdo, because I think she'll think I'm a liar.
>
> Finally, what can I do? I did it because I had reason. I saw what I started. May God pardon that person. I prayed for her, so that she doesn't fall any lower. Yesterday my pain was so great that I became ill. During the night I was almost agonizing, but Jesus and my Mother consoled me. I'm suffering this for Him. Such was the impression I had on seeing people so deficient, that I doubted my vocation because I thought it was all hypocrisy. But Jesus said to me that I must not be surprised, since one of His apostles had fallen,

> and that I should pray for her. They, the other girls at school, told me all kinds of things that made me believe that all was lost. They even told me things that Mother Izquierdo was thinking about me. Then I became very upset, since I had said this to prevent a Nun from giving bad example. Finally, may God's will be done. What does the opinion of creatures matter?[35]

Both Mother Rios and Mother Izquierdo thought highly of her, so it was a shock to Juanita to think she had fallen in their estimation of her. In her humility she wanted to put the incident down in writing to show how imperfect she was, 'a criminal nothingness', in her own phrase. On the other hand, she did have a tendency to need the approval of others, so it was also a lesson in humility for her. She then described another instance when her humility was tested, when she lost her self-control over the small incident of a bee:

> I want to leave in writing an event that happened. Even though it's small it served to humiliate me. We were in class when a bee or another larger insect came near me. Without knowing how, in one leap I got out of the room; afterward, I was so ashamed of not having known how to conquer myself. But I finally offered the humiliation to God and came back into the room. Mother Izquierdo then looked at me with such a fixed and profound stare that I wished the ground would swallow me up as I was remembering the little control I have over my inclinations. Oh, I see myself so little and so miserable. I was alone. Jesus left me and I, without Jesus, what am I but misery? Afterward I went to ask Mother Izquierdo's pardon. I confess that it cost me, but I directed myself to my Mother Mary and she, as always, helped me. Mother Izquierdo immediately said it was all right. I think I'd have preferred to have her scold me. Then I recalled Jesus and His Mercy, when He looked at Peter and made his heart tender through His gaze. I thanked God for this event, since I didn't offend Him, but it served to humiliate me.[36]

Nevertheless, the nuns did have a high regard for Juanita and in August she was given more responsibility, not only looking after the little girls, but also taking charge of a recreation class. 'I'm happy, since it's a proof of on the part of Reverend Mother. I felt a little vanity, but I rejected it and spoke to Jesus'.

Looking after the younger children, Juanita proved to be a born teacher. Children have an instinct to know whether love is genuine or not and knowing that Juanita's love for them was genuine, they loved her dearly in return; but they were not above teasing her, especially because of the loving relationship she had with them. They mischievously called her *Mater Admirabilis*, 'Mother Most Admirable', which was a special devotion to Our Lady of the Sacred Heart Sisters. She herself had a special devotion to this title of Our Lady; does her meditation of it, explain a little bit, of what the little girls instinctively recognised in Juanita herself?

> Today I contemplated *Mater Admirabilis* in the temple, in that majestic silence whereby she united her whole being to God. In this way she went about adoring Him and recognizing her nothingness before God. I tried to keep recollected and remained as long as I could with my eyes lowered and in the presence of Jesus.[37]

Her graceful bearing and height, as well as her – usual! - self-possession and evident goodness, made this a fitting description for Juanita, but, just as when she was little, her playmates had tried to provoke her to anger, so the little girls tried to provoke her and break through her goodness, once successfully:

> The little girls teased me so much in class that I finally began to cry. I had a headache and my back ached so that I didn't know what was happening to me. I didn't answer them because I didn't want to break the silence. I offered it to the good Jesus. But then, at recess time I told them they should go to the other side of the room,

> that they shouldn't tease me so much. Then I almost became angry, but afterward we made up very nicely and in the afternoon they sent me a holy card. It cost me dearly to put up with the teasing; but the little ones told me that I have a very good temperament and, because I don't get angry but go along with the teasing, they do it to me. Each day I feel that they love me more and this is because I give them good example.[38]

When they realized they had really upset her on this occasion, though, they gave her the holy card by way of apology.

There was little time for Juanita to write in her diary for a while then, due to the busy school term, but in a worrying development she continued to be dogged by ill health, which was getting worse, writing in her diary 27th August:

> I don't know what's happening to me, since I continually feel exhausted. Today at different times I've had to use all my strength of will not to permit myself to be overcome by sadness. Yesterday I made this resolution in my meditation: to be cheerful all day long. There were times I was almost unable to break out of this exhaustion of soul in which I found myself. I believe that it's the weakness I find in myself: a constant headache. And add to this the pain in my back. I don't know how I feel: but I'm happy, since I'm suffering.[39]

She was too ill to be able to go to Communion for several days, and it was decided to take her out of school for a while to recuperate. It gave her the time to at last write to the Los Andes Carmel, introducing herself to Mother Angelica. She was wearing a medal the Prioress had given her: 'The little medal I wear constantly is doubly precious because it comes from my dear Carmel, since you already know, through Chela, Rev. Mother, the love and esteem that I have for the Carmelites and the desire I cherish of some day counting myself among them'.[40] She is honest about her poor health; she leaves that in Our Lady's hands, but she is sure of what a Carmelite vocation entails:

> I also know that if I go to Carmel it will be to suffer, but suffering is nothing new or unknown to me.. In it I find my joy, for Jesus is on the cross and He is love. And what does suffering matter if a person loves? The life of a Carmelite is one of suffering, loving and praying, and I find my whole ideal in this, Rev. Mother. My Jesus has taught me these three things since I was a little girl.[41]

In her letter Juanita asks the Prioress to keep the news of her vocation a secret, because she had revealed it only to a few close friends and, crucially, her mother. She was greatly encouraged to receive a swift and encouraging reply. The Prioress included in her letter a holy card of Our Lady and a medal.

By the end of September Juanita was well enough to enjoy some outings during the school holidays, as she wrote to her father; the only shadow being that he was not there with them:

> We've gone on many outings. Sunday we went with five girls to Don Ricardo Salas' farm. Since we had to spend the whole day there, none of the women could go. But Mom offered to take us all. We left at 1.30 p.m. on the train from Pirque and got off at Bellavista, which is the first station. There Don Ricardo's little girls were waiting for us. They had sent an automobile for us, which was wonderful but, since we didn't all fit in, some went by horse-drawn carriages that belonged to the farm. It took us ten minutes to get from the station to the house. We had a wonderful trip. That day the farm hands celebrated September Eighteenth [Chile's Independence Day]; that's why Don Ricardo had organized an entertainment for them: elevation balloons, fireworks, donkey rides, etc.
>
> They have a magnificent tennis court. In short, we enjoyed the

whole day. We thought of you, Daddy, because you would have loved to see the farm. It's very pretty. You can see green pastures everywhere and lots of water.

Tomorrow we're going to the School of Aviation with Chiro, who's a friend of one of the School officials. I think we're going up in a plane. I'd love to go up in a plane and land in San Javier to go give you a big hug and a kiss. What do you think, Dad?[42]

She gave her father news of the seven-year-old Ignatio, who was now able to walk without his cane after his accident more than a year ago. Miguel had gone out with Chiro in the hopes of landing a job, she said, and then adds, 'Lucita and Chiro continue to be rather unconcerned, as you know, and especially now that Chiro is on vacation. You can imagine how happy they are'.

Chico, Isidore Huneeus Guzmán, was an officer in the Chilean Army, and the pair were trying to hide, what was obvious to everyone, that they were deeply in love.

At the turn of the century the world was moving into a new era: motor cars taking over from horse-drawn carriages, planes taking to the skies. As she never mentioned it, Juanita probably didn't manage to go up in an aeroplane.

Juanita went to confession 11 September and spoke to the priest a long time about her vocation. In the course of her confession, the priest gave her advice that would be of great value to people drawn to the Carmelite charism and searching for ways in which to put it into practice in their own lives.

He gave her suggestions as to the different ways people are called to a Carmelite vocation, including how to be a 'Carmelite in the world'. Some feel they have a vocation, but trying it in the cloister are unable to follow the austerity of Carmel and leave. It is a consolation to them to know that their time in Carmel was not wasted but was in the Lord's will for them. The good news is that the Carmelite charism, in its simplicity, can easily be followed in the world:

He told me that as far as he could see, for now, I have a true vocation to be a Carmelite. Jesus might give me a vocation that is permanent, that is to say, forever, and I could enter Carmel. Or, He might give me a transitory or momentary vocation to free me from all evil in body or soul. Also, I must be true to my vocation, follow it if God gives me the necessary qualities. Also, to be a Carmelite spiritually, that is to say, follow the Carmelite way of life in my own home by getting up at a certain time, making an hour of meditation and then going to Mass, taking Communion and returning home and starting work. I'd be in the presence of God all day long, and at night I could make another hour of meditation. Then I'd go to bed at a fixed time and visit as little as possible.[43]

The priest was not the only one to be doubtful as to her vocation to the enclosed Order. She went to have an interview with Mother Izquierdo at the end of term, who once again told her she had no vocation or the health to be a Carmelite. This might explain why at one point Juanita noticed a certain coldness in the sister's attitude to her. Perhaps she was disappointed that despite her warnings Juanita still wanted to enter Carmel; she would not become a Sacred Heart Sister, for which she was admirably suited, as Mother Izquierdo would surely have been thinking, that with her intelligence and love for children, what an excellent teacher she would have made.

At the end of October, the 29th, there was a recreation day for the lay Sisters, the Sacred Heart Sisters who carried out the domestic work around the school, and the Children of Mary took their place, as Juanita said, 'performing the office of Martha'. The previous day she had taken part in a procession in honour of the Infant of Prague, whose statue is venerated by the Carmelites, organized by the Carmelite Fathers of Santiago; she was praying for a miracle of healing for Ignacio's injured leg. They didn't receive the miracle, but Juanita was delighted that her father was there, taking part in the procession.

When the term ended Juanita went back home, clutching prizes and medals she had won, but the one she cherished most was the medal of a Child of Mary.

Their father was unable to be at home for Christmas, so a few days later Juanita shared all their news with him. Both she and Rebecca had done well in their exams and received prizes. Luis took all the honours in his class. 'We were thinking of you when they announced his prizes at the University, because you would have enjoyed seeing him given so many prizes. A father is always happy with the success of his children'.[44]

On the 25th we went to the gymnastic parade at the Military School. It was performed with admirable precision. But Chiro did not command his unit. They showed a riding school class who performed several jumping exercises and a few exercises with their swords drawn, executing them without a single mistake. Another class was on gymnastics. They did a formation squadron, jumping about two meters. Finally, for the closing, they sang a very pretty hymn.[45]

Once the Christmas festivities were over, the family prepared once more for their holidays. Sadly, the hacienda at Chacabulco had had to be sold, and they had to look for an alternative, something less expensive than Chacabulco would have been.

CHAPTER SIX
Dear Old Algorrobo

The family spent their holidays instead in Algarrobo, which was then only a small seaside village. Friends of theirs, the Lyons family, had a beach home where they stayed. Life there was much more primitive, but the village and its surroundings soon won Juanita's heart. While describing life in Algorrobo, already she is looking through the beauty of the earth to see the Creator of it, and opening herself to the Infinite, as she wrote to Carmen Ortuzar:

> Here life goes along very pleasantly. We have an enchanting coastline here. We live in a house that's right on the beach, about three meters from the ocean. As you can guess, we have a delightful view. Everything I tell you about how easy going life is here will be too little. Here people dress as they like. The girls wear straw hats; it's all like that. On the beach you see a group of only about four or five women and 11 girls gathered around them. We go swimming together. You can go about a block into the water up to your neck, and with no need to avoid waves or currents, because there are none. You can swim better here than in a swimming pool …
>
> One day we went on horseback riding with Teresa Lyon. You can't imagine a more beautiful landscape than the one we saw: huge waterfalls between two mountains, covered with trees, and at the end of them, an opening through which one can see the ocean, above which clouds of different colours were reflected, and behind that, an overcast sun. You couldn't imagine anything more beautiful because it makes me think of the God who created such a beautiful earth, even if it is a place of sorrow. What can Heaven be like – I often ask myself – when it's about enjoyment? …

> I haven't told you anything about the town Algarrobo. Their houses except for two or three are truly those of the poor: piles of bricks, beamed roofs, and no furniture. It's amusing to see how surprised people are who come to see the famous town. Our little house, though poor, is comfortable. It has all the furniture we need and plenty of rooms. People forgive everything because of the trust here and because of the view we've got …
>
> Last night was an ideal night. We went outside and sat on the sand. It was the first time the moon could be seen, since every day it had clouded up at night. It would be impossible to describe anything more perfect. I felt that you were right there beside me. Carmen, does it ever happen to you that when you're looking at the ocean you feel a longing for the infinite? We feel in our soul an inexplicable loneliness, that only God can fill, because everything seems so very small.[46]

She also wrote to her father, giving him news of all they were doing, including swimming in the sea. They were near the Nano river so went to bathe there first, perhaps to reassure little Ignacio, who became frightened about going in. There were plenty of other things to do:

> We've had lots of hikes and trips on horseback and on foot and a carriage ride that I believe Lucita mentioned to you. Yesterday we had a trip that was beautiful and comfortable for everyone since it was just girls. We organised an outing with Miss Julia Friere de Rivas, since we're all close friends of her daughter. There were 11 of us in all who went to have lunch at a waterfall called Las Petras. There's a huge forest where not a ray of sunshine gets in, and where the finest and most precious ferns grow like weeds. We had a very delicious lunch and afterwards one of the girls sang. Then we began to play a game of 'steal the bacon'. In short, we had such a good time that the afternoon just flew by.
>
> We also went on hikes, taking trips through canyons with Luz Friere's governess. You can't imagine what wonderful views we

saw all along the way. The fields were pretty and in full regalia, and from a distance the sea looked like a lake. Our favourite outings were to the sand dunes that little Ignacia loves so much, because there we get to jump down almost 3 metres from them, rolling around and around.[47]

In Algorrobo, also, the family organized events for the people, but this vacation was more for a rest for them all, without a Mission, although Juanita still wanted to run a catechism class for the children. 'Here they have two Masses, but today we had four and, in the afternoon every day we have benediction. We with the Lyon girls have formed a musical choir, which would not be too bad if they knew how to accompany us. Today we're going to look for some girls for a catechism course with Gabriela Lyon.'[48]

'Juanita had great zeal for teaching catechism' said Teresa Lyon, another daughter of the family, 'and her zeal sprung from her faith in God. Juanita spent a summer vacation at my home in Algarrobo and I saw her with the children who were very undisciplined – some of them, children of alcoholics – and Juanita used to teach them the basic truths of their faith with great patience. She was heroic because she sacrificed her vacations in this difficult apostolate of teaching catechism and in the way she would exercise the apostolate, that is with patience and perseverance.'[49]

With her thoughts continually on the Los Andes Carmel, Juanita told Mother Angelica that her holiday reading was the *Way of Perfection* as well as the *Autobiography of St Teresa of Avila*. The beauty of her surroundings led her to contemplation of the beauty of God, echoing St Elizabeth of the Trinity who wrote to her Rolland aunts: 'Can't you feel me there among you in that dear Carlipa with its beautiful Serre? But the horizons of Carmel are even more beautiful, it is the infinite,'[50] something that Juanita totally agreed with, writing to the Prioress:

> Everything I see, Rev. Mother, draws me to God. The ocean, with its immensity makes me think of God and of His infinite grandeur. It's then that I feel a thirst for the infinite. When I think of how when I become a Carmelite, God willing, I'll have to abandon all this, I tell Our Lord that I find all beauty and all greatness in Him. But in the world everything's so small, passing, and the only thing I want is Jesus.[51]

She was grateful, too, to know that she wouldn't have to wait two years from leaving school before entering Carmel, as she had been led to believe, 'because I think that even if I had to walk through fire, I'd pass through it with Jesus, if I'm well enough to go this year. Pray a lot for this intention. I'm going to begin a novena to Mater Admirabilis for this goal, because it's my health that frightens me. Now, despite being at the shore, the doctor finds me very weak. What should I do, Rev. Mother? If Jesus wants me to become a Carmelite, He'll give me the health for it. May His will be done.'[52]

As always, they went horseback riding and had lots of fun flying kites and playing tricks. As Juanita described in her entry for Sunday 18th their cousins, who were in the presbytery, were trying to distract them while the family were at Mass. 'This was very trying. We sang, but I was not proud nor did I desire to draw attention to myself', Juanita added, because she had a beautiful and strong contralto voice. 'Jesus helped me in this to overcome myself. I give Him thanks with my whole heart.'[53]

However, Juanita's health wasn't so good, writing to her friend Carmen, 'As for my health, I can tell you I'm about the same. I always have a lot of pain in my chest, which caused my mother to take me to a doctor who said that it was because of my high-strung temperament and that everything comes from that anaemia of mine.'[54]

In fact, her own doctor had diagnosed her problem as anaemia. The pain in her chest and shoulder was caused by a nerve running up from her kidneys. Her prescribed her medicine which cured the problem and he advised her to always wear something warm next to her kidneys.

The holiday was a rest for them, but also filled with the many outings they took. In a letter to her father she describes the picnics, the horse-riding, and evening entertainment, so it is not surprising that she felt unwell. She described the friends there as worldly, and an evening at Julia Feire's home as boring, so with her longing for Carmel it was sometimes a strain for her. Nevertheless, her enjoyment of life was unfeigned and she put other's enjoyment first however she felt. Isabel Espinoz Labarca, another schoolfriend, said:

> More than once Juanita visited my home. She took the guitar and struck up some Chilean dance tunes. She had a good contralto voice and used to sing our Chilean songs joyfully. She made much over the tenants' children and added to their healthy good time. She organized gunny sack competitions and donkey races and gave sweets or some religious gift to the winners. Juanita ended up covered with dirt from the games, and she was the most joyful and enthusiastic.[55]

In fact, playing the guitar for others to dance to was a quiet ploy of Juanita. There is a photo of her with friends and all the young women have dresses buttoned to the neck, but in the evenings they were likely to dress with much lower necklines. Juanita, mindful of the vow of chastity she had taken when she was fifteen, and mindful of her desire to enter Carmel, preferred not to dress in what could be a provocative way and join in the exuberant dancing. To play the guitar was her way of choosing an alternative that would not in any way make her stand out or make others feel embarrassed but instead gave them pleasure.

Juanita's preference for dressing modestly and without jewellery didn't always meet with her mother's approval. One day, when they were due to go out visiting, Doña Lucia became angry and made her put on a more suitable dress. Juanita said nothing and simply changed her clothes as her mother wished.

Whether in school or on holiday, those who were with her never guessed that she was weary with her surroundings. She might have preferred the silence of the cloister or a quiet time before the Blessed Sacrament, but in fact these quiet times were all of a piece of her love of life in all its aspects. 'Once she was invited to my parent's ranch on September 18th', her school friend, Elena Salas Pereira, said. 'Juanita brought joy to all the tenants at Viña Tarapaca. She rode horseback very well. She was a skillful amazon. During recess periods at school, she stood out for her friendliness and sweetness.'[56]

The social gatherings at the house of another friend, Luz de Rivas, were not what she would have chosen. 'From everything I saw and heard, I've got a very poor impression of their social events,' she confided to Carmen. 'I ask myself how they can call that kind of entertainment where nothing goes but pure foolishness.'[57] She admitted to Carmen that some of the girls in their social circle were not her type, but she joined in nevertheless. As another friend, Maria Guzmán, affirmed, Juanita was 'of a joyful temperament and fun loving'.[58]

The Friere de Rivas were non-religious freethinkers, but they were drawn to Juanita's unobtrusive holiness. Julia, their mother, often had discussions with Juanita about the writings of St Teresa of Avila and St John of the Cross, remarking 'You people don't know what a treasure getting to know that girl has been for me.'[59] As for Juanita, she wrote to Mother Angelica that her desire to enter the 'little heaven' of Carmel was growing ever stronger. 'All the more now that I'm so much with worldly people. I've seen that happiness doesn't exist in the world and dealing with the world always leaves an emptiness that Our Lord fills completely when I'm with Him in church'.[60]

Juanita returned to school for what she had decided with her mother would be her last term. They left 'dear old Algorrobo' with 'floods of tears coming from our eyes, you could have formed a sea the size of Algorrobo'. She would be leaving when she was just turned eighteen, a year earlier than was usual, even after being reassured that she wouldn't have to wait two years before entering Carmel. And the return to school? 'How terrible! I can feel goosebumps!'

CHAPTER SEVEN
Farewell To School

Back at school for the last time, Juanita's health was still giving her problems, with pains in her chest and shoulder. 'Everything looks so bad, because I won't become a Carmelite if my health is so bad'.[61] and her prayer was bad, too, leaving her feeling that Jesus had abandoned her; this played out in her school life with her emotions in turmoil:

> I'm in a terrible state ... Angry. With desires to be mischievous. Mad at the nuns. Without taste for prayer, because I encounter dryness in it. I feel despondent. At each moment I'm failing in my duties. And Jesus told me today that it was because I was attached to creatures. I want to be loved by them. I cry because I don't know what is happening to me and I have no one to counsel me or help me. Mother Izquierdo was angry, and that is tormenting me.[62]

Some of her problems would have been caused by the tension of her longing for Carmel and yet afraid her health would never permit it. Her desires to overcome herself yet seeing that, in her eyes, she was failing Jesus. She wanted to take on 'mortifications' such as wearing a hair shirt, which Fr Blanch did allow on occasion, but with her health so poor now she was not allowed to do so. She was learning that it was the trials that the Lord permitted that cost the most, rather than things she might herself want to do.

The response of Jesus was that she should always carry out His will with joy, even though her spirits were low. 'That I may remain in peace, I shouldn't look at the future. I want to keep this maxim before me'.[63]

Juanita

She was still having problems in her relations with Mother Izquierdo, and this was teaching her another lesson. Juanita had a loving and affectionate nature and longed to receive affection and love in return. But Jesus was teaching her not to rely on the approval of others, but seek approval only from Him who alone knows the human heart:

> Mother Izquierdo is angry with me. I don't know what I have done. She's not the same mother toward me she used to be. I continue to have the same affection and trust toward her. This frightens my soul. Why, my Jesus, are You placing this sadness around my heart? Ah, it is because You love me. You want to encircle me only with Your love so that I will not be attached to any creature.[64]

In her innocence, Juanita might not have realised that Mother Izquierdo was battling with the same problem. During Juanita's schooldays, would she not have become very fond of her outstanding and dearly loved student and was now having to accept that she would have to let Juanita go from her forever, entering Carmel rather than the Sacred Heart Sisters?

In the darkness and dryness of her prayer, Juanita was having doubts as to whether it was really Jesus who was speaking to her, and, if it was truly He, then He should inspire Mother Izquierdo to ask of her this question: 'Do you love Christ?' The following day the nun came up to her and asked her that very question. Juanita blushed with emotion and remained silent, and Mother Izquerdo added, 'And are you not answering with all your soul?'

'It would be monstrous if I did not love Him' Juanita replied; the sister then understood the depths of Juanita's love for God and Juanita received the assurance she needed. [65]

It was decided that Juanita would leave school in August, and the school that once gave her goosebumps was now a beloved school that she could barely think to leave. Jesus asked her not to cry leaving the school and Juanita replied that it would make her look unappreciative -but that showed her attachment to what others thought of her, was the reply of Jesus; it was just another chain from which she needed to free herself.

Rebecca would still be at school, and Juanita was acutely aware of how her younger sister would feel the loss, without her older sister there to help her. 'The poor little thing! I assure you that it breaks my heart to see how she's suffering', she wrote to a classmate, Elena. 'The thought of separation is troubling her more than it should, for, as you know, she's aware of everything'. Rebecca would need a confidante to replace her sister, 'And that angel of consolation is going to be you', decided Juanita.[66] Elena should do this discreetly, in a fair exchange, while Juanita would keep Elena's secret, that she was intending to enter the Sacred Heart Sisters.

Juanita made a retreat before leaving school, 'heavenly days', and now the day of parting was almost upon her:

> I'm leaving school. It's impossible to describe what I'm suffering. Oh, my God, how everything passes away and comes to an end! How much we attach ourselves to what's transitory. I haven't cried, but my heart is torn to pieces ... Farewell, Sisters, who have taught me the way of virtue, who have shown me the road to complete happiness here on earth and the way to heaven. Farewell, dwelling place of the Heart of Jesus, where for three years I have lived with You. Farewell, my dear companions. Your affection will always live in my memory. Farewell, farewell, everyone. I'm going to Him. I'm going to Him and I'll be happy. I won't cry. With generosity I want to make my sacrifice to God. All for You, Jesus, until death.[67]

Juanita was true to her promise: she left dry-eyed but with her heart breaking, to begin another stage in her life.

CHAPTER EIGHT
I'm Famous For My Fits Of Laughter

How many different impressions I'm experiencing! Sadness because I'm leaving my beloved school as well as the Sisters and my companions, to whom I am so grateful. How good they are to me, what affection they show me, although I was so unworthy of that! I carried out my sacrifice without crying. Truly, I felt a strength in myself that was superior to my own; it was Jesus who made me so strong in that instant. I felt my heart was being destroyed when I said farewell to my life as a student, but I didn't cry because I had promised our Lord to prepare myself for the great sacrifice I must accomplish in a few months. On the other hand, I feel the attractiveness of home life, of life with my family that I had abandoned when I was so young; of returning to a life of intimacy with my own in order to do good and to sacrifice myself for each one of them at every moment …

My heart is also seized with fear. An unknown path is opening before my eyes, and the unknown always produces distrust. On top of that, I'm going to enter the world, that world so perverse. I'm going to be submerged in a cold atmosphere, glacial in its social indifference. Will I succumb to it? God alone knows what I've suffered! Over and above that, the Sisters at school believed I was leaving because I wanted to. How far I am from doing my own will. Circumstances forced me to leave my dear little school, that refuge of peace, innocence and joy. It was, above everything, God's will that was urgently calling me. Today, I now find myself in the world and see what my life is. I find that life in God can be continued even more than in the school. How many sacrifices that are unknown to all! Besides, my life is more prayerful. I spend a lot of time alone in my room with God alone. Study used to take up my thoughts much more. Now I must think only of Him.[68]

Despite her apprehensions, Juanita found her new life easier than she had expected. She was able to give her days some structure, with time for prayer, which was so essential to her, and was finding that what seemed to her to be a mystery while at school was now unfolding peacefully. Juanita had implied that leaving school early wasn't her desire; one of the reasons why it was her mother's wish was because she wanted Juanita with her, so that after her sister, Lucia's, marriage to Chico in June, she wanted Juanita to take over the management of the household from her. Her mother didn't make the task easy for her, as Juanita wrote to Fr Blanch. But even in this mundane situation she gave it a spiritual significance, seeing Our Lord's will in this and as a means to keep her humble. To kiss the ground was a Carmelite practice when corrected for a fault:

> I don't have time to do my household chores. I didn't believe that life at home would be a life of sacrifice. Believe me, Rev. Father, it has served as a preparation for my religious life. My mother is constantly giving me orders and scolding me that I don't do things well. And often times for no good reason. I don't know how to thank Our Lord, for in this way He's inspiring my mother so that I may always live on the cross, which is a proof of His love. How dearly it sometimes costs me to keep silent! And when I answer back, I've decided to kiss the ground to humble myself and beg my mother's forgiveness. I'm also striving to obey my inferiors, as Our Lord did at Nazareth.[69]

Now, she took the most important step, to write to Mother Angelica and ask for formal permission to enter the Los Andes Carmel, even before she had visited it:

> Rev. Mother, right now I plead with you to admit me to that little dovecote nest. I know that I'm not worthy, my dear Mother, of this great favour; but, believe me, I'll work my whole life long to become a great saint. Saint Teresa says that it's not pride to

espouse lofty desires, quite the contrary, this will lift the soul to the most sublime things.⁷⁰

To her delight Juanita received a swift, affirmative reply:

> You can't imagine how well your letters are attuned to my needs and the great joy they bring me, especially your latest one where you tell me that there's an 'opening' for this poor and miserable girl in that very dear dovecote. How I thanked my Lord from the bottom of my soul when I read the lines that brought me this happiest of news. Believe me, I feel exiled in this world, amidst so many dangers, and long to see myself already in that little convent, an eternal prisoner of Our Lord; and I have no other thought, desire or occupation that is not directed to Him.⁷¹

In the meantime, she prepared herself for Carmel and the little cell that would be hers, by living more and more in the cell within her soul. This was a practice beloved of St Elizabeth of the Trinity. Without this inward preparation, her cell in Carmel would be empty:

> I keep myself closely united to Our Lord within the home of my soul; so, that has to be my little cell for now. Whenever I go out on the street or to the theatre or take a walk, I tell Our Lord: 'My Jesus, although perhaps no one here is thinking about You, but here's a heart that belongs completely to You. I adore \you, I love You. Make me Yours always'. In this way I keep myself recollected and removed from worldly things.⁷²

Juanita went to stay with the Valdès Ossa family and their two daughters Herminia (Chubby) and Elisita (Eli) at the end of the year. She wrote to Rebecca, who had stayed in Santiago, still studying in the elementary school she had been to first. She went horseback riding and took trips in the family car. Herminia and Elisa were her cousins and great friends. The family had organised a Mission with the Redemptorist Fathers and the three girls helped out, teaching catechism, visiting the families. It was a great success, as she told Rebecca:

> You don't know, my dear little Dove, how I keep thinking about you and how anxious I am to see you. You, who, more than anyone, needs good country air to regain new strength, find yourself shut up there in Santiago. How you would enjoy being driven at full speed along these splendid roads which are magnificently shaded, and also listening to the German tales told with such grace by the priest.
>
> The Mission results here were splendid. Never before had I witnessed such a touching scene than on the night on the Feast of Reparation. Imagine them all, begging forgiveness aloud; but in in the beginning the men didn't do it. Then the priest spoke to the children and they began to ask their fathers to forgive them. And soon the women followed and finally everybody began crying, and two of the women fainted. Then Chubby began to laugh. That was pathetic, I can assure you.[73]

Juanita wrote to her mother, also, giving her more news. It was no surprise that Chubby burst out laughing during the Mission service, because they were enjoying themselves greatly:

> We spent three days on our own. And the two of us with Herminia entertained ourselves. The other day we went out for a walk; and, since we had to cross the river, we climbed on a horse and cart on which we crossed the river. We took a trip to go and explore the farm; but, since it was a little rough, we didn't get very far but went back where they laughed a lot at our plans. Chubby was in a little cart, and I did the driving. We went off to inspect the houses

of Don Ismael Valdès, which are beautiful and have a lovely park, although the one here is nicer.

> During the month of Mary [Advent] we pray every evening. Eli does the prayer of the month, and I pray the rosary and play the organ. Can you imagine that yesterday we were singing an 'Ave Maria' and Herminia tried to get us to laugh. Instead of singing, we began to howl. We couldn't go on.[74]

For all the laughter and jokes, Juanita was coming into ever greater union with God. That the Los Andes Prioress had given her consent to her entry into Carmel would explain her joy. She was also able to talk in depth to Elisita, who was also wanting to enter the religious life, with the Sacred Heart Sisters. She gave more details of the Mission in a letter to Mother Angelica, as well as the more serious side of her stay there:

> I've been staying on Eli's farm for 26 days, and thank God there were only 6 days when I was unable to go to Mass, though we did make spiritual Communion. How good Our Lord is to those who love Him! How many heavenly days, my dearest Mother, we spent together before the tabernacle. When I was at the foot of the tabernacle, I had the happiness of finding myself alone with the infinite God who is imprisoned for love of us …
>
> The two of us with Eli were the sacristans, and every night we would go to prepare the tabernacle light and leave Him our hearts for the whole night. I remember that we were determined not to leave Him and sometimes made about five genuflexions without being ready to leave Him alone all night long …
>
> There were ore than1,300 Communions, 70 First Communions, baptisms, confirmations and weddings. Truly it was a very fruitful Mission, thanks to the God who moved their hearts.[75]

She entertained her sister with news of their exploits and their fun:

> I've become famous for my fits of laughter ... we've done nothing but kid around. Prepare yourself. We are the last ones at table with Pepe. We've told so many jokes and laughed so much that sometimes I can't eat. And the most tragic part of it was that the priest who said grace after the meal had to stop his prayer halfway through. He was unable to continue because of the laughter and because we infected him with our laughter.
>
> In the morning Herminia comes to wake me up with water and chairs, a blanket and everything she finds along her way and throw it all at me on top of the bed. So during the day I get even, and at night I don't let her sleep. And I want you to know that she beds down very early.[76]

On her return to Santiago, and as she entered a new year, a new and unexpected trial awaited her.

CHAPTER NINE

That Dovecote Nest

The next trial came from a most unexpected place: 'Christ brought me His cross as a Christmas gift', Juanita wrote in her diary. Perhaps it was from nostalgia for her school days, but she suddenly had her doubts as to whether she should enter the Carmelites or the Sacred Heart Sisters. During her visit to the Mother Vicar before she left school, the nun had given her an intimate understanding of the life of a Sacred Heart Sister; as Juanita summarized it: it is a mixed life of prayer and action; they must live a very deep interior life, since they must keep God within themselves and yet give Him to souls. They must always remain with Him.

This would, of course, have resonated strongly with Juanita, and she knew from experience, from seeing the life of the Sacred Heart Sisters up close, how dedicated they were to their vocation of giving themselves totally to their young charges. 'They live by seeing comforts but without possessing them', which again would have resonated with Juanita's desire for poverty.

On the other hand, Jesus had, since she was fourteen, told her that her vocation was to be a Carmelite: 'When I'm in prayer Our Lord tells me that He has chosen me for that life which is so perfect and so filled with union with Himself because He love me greatly among those chosen by His Divine Heart'.[77]

She wrote candidly to both Fr Blanch and to Mother Angelica about her doubts. The Prioress must have been quite shocked about this after already accepting Juanita to enter with them. The only solution was for her to visit the Los Andes Carmel and see for herself.

In January, everything seemed to work for Juanita and her mother to at last be able to visit the Los Andes Carmel. Miguel had gone with his father to the farm, only Rebecca and Ignacio were at home with them, so her mother packed the two children off for the day, leaving it clear for herself and Juanita to make the 60-mile journey to the Carmel.

As soon as Juanita saw the poor, run-down little house she was immediately drawn to it. 'When I saw my dear little convent, what an impact it made on me!' she wrote to her friend Elena Gonzales. 'It looks so poor! It doesn't look like a convent but like an old house. Still its poverty speaks so well of it. I had barely caught sight of it when its poverty won me over and seduced me.'[78]

She had already visited the Carmel in Santiago but was not attracted to it. One reason she gave was that the extern sister began talking about secular things and people in a way that Juanita thought was inappropriate. It perhaps, also, didn't have the air of radical poverty that she was seeking.

She was seeking something more, she was seeking somewhere far distant from the world. In seeing the remote little Los Andes Carmel, where news would be sparse, she knew she had found her home. She understood that her particular vocation was to cut herself of as far as possible from the outside world so that she would be wholly oriented towards her Lord, in intense contemplative prayer and intercessory prayer.

It was her 'particular vocation', for even contemplative Carmelites are not all called to that level of intensity and radical detachment from the world to which Juanita felt herself called. For some, their intercessory prayer means having some knowledge of external events going on in the world and individual requests for prayer. Other contemplatives feel that there is no need for such knowledge because their gaze is fixed on God, who allows His grace to flow through them to where the need is. Both are valid, and in practice both intertwine, for when intercession is directed to Our Lord, the one who prays will know that mostly the results of that prayer will be known only when they are in heaven.

Juanita continued with her description of the Community, enchanted by their informality:

There are 16 sisters, 18 counting the two externs, and we bantered as though we'd always known one another. They have great simplicity, trust and intimacy. They joked among themselves and laughed. And this was the case from the lowest postulant to M Angelica ... they're enchanting, so joyful and informal.[79]

Teresa went to pray in the chapel for a short while and there received confirmation from the Lord himself that this was indeed where He wanted her to be. 'I saw Our Lord with a smiling face, and it seemed that He said He was happy there, listening to the praises of His brides.'[80]

Mother Angelica also confirmed her vocation, saying that from receiving the very first letter from her, she had known that Juanita was a born Carmelite.

The Carmel of Los Andes that Juanita aspired to enter was a fairly recent foundation. The presence of contemplative orders in Chile and the South Americas at the time of Teresa of Los Andes was fairly recent, because when missionaries first came to these countries the Missionary Orders were felt to be most important. Then, when the Faith was established, there came the need for contemplative orders such as the Carmelites.

The Carmel had been founded in 1898 by Mother Margaret of St John of the Cross from the Santiago Carmel that Juanita had felt was not the one for her. Mother Margaret brought with her Mother Angelica Teresa of the Most Blessed Sacrament from the Curimon Carmel to be the Prioress. She was a holy and gifted Carmelite, so she would be an excellent guide for Juanita, or, to give her the name that Mother Angelica had decided would be hers in Carmel, Sr Teresa of Jesus. This humbled and delighted Juanita, that she would have such an illustrious name to live up to. The Los Andes kept the Carmelite rule in great fidelity and austerity. It was indeed poor and run-down, as Juanita described, without any hot running water, no electricity and no hygiene facilities.

When the family went shortly afterwards for an extended stay on a farm her father was renting at San Pablo, Juanita's thoughts were full of Camel, happy now that her vocation was fixed and her mind at peace, writing to Mother Angelica: 'I'm still rejoicing over my visit to the little convent, and I remain continually in union with it, longing more and more to come and cloister myself here and serve my dear sisters, even if I'm to occupy the last place. Because to serve the Sisters is what suits me most, though I'm the least worthy of it.'[81]

Juanita found it difficult to find time for prayer because she was with the rest of the family all the time, so she prayed during the night and began reading St John of the Cross.

As usual, the family arranged for a Mission for the local people and estate workers, as she write to Elisa Ossa:

> The Heart of Mary Fathers came from Talca. They're excellent missionaries and very enthusiastic. The people were delighted, and all the more so since they'd never seen Missions given on such a grand scale here. The people at all cost wanted to go and take the priests to the train station.
>
> The two of us, with Rebecca, taught catechism. More than 50 children were here; and, after the Missions we went on teaching class every day. The people here know very little. It seems that they're being taught little or nothing at the public school ...
>
> The people here are lots of fun because they're not used to others running things, since almost all are property holders and people put on airs among them; so they were delighted when we dealt with them the way we did. They called my mother the doctor lady. You can't imagine the fame they brought her, because they came to her with a little boy, dying from a wound that covered his whole head. You could see down to the bone. We all thought he was going to die, because he was deathly ill. My mother gave him an injection, bandaged him up and in less than a month's time, he has fully regained his health.[82]

Once the Mission was over, the stay in San Pablo was peaceful: 'I've hardly been able to go riding at all. I keep reading, and in the evenings we go for a walk. And we often go down to the banks of the Maule River where there's such a lovely view.' [83] She joined the others in going round the different houses, consecrating the homes to the Sacred Heart.

Juanita asked the Carmel to send her samples of the material and pattern for the postulant's dress she would need. Since she hadn't been able to speak to her father yet, she hid the parcel until she and Rebecca could make an excuse to take a trip into town. Rebecca wore the apron under her dress and Juanita the waistcoat, giggling at the conspiracy of it all, then they went to a remote spot in the nearby pine forest to try on the garments. After trying them on, Juanita had to write to the Prioress to say that the garments were too wide and too short for her and asked her to send some alternatives.

At the beginning of March she journeyed with Luis to Bucalemu to stay with their aunt and uncle Ruiz-Tagle on their beautiful estate there. The intrepid Juanita was able to enjoy horse riding to the full in the stunning countryside, as she write to Rebecca:

> The Rapel River has the most lovely scenery. The river flows through mountains covered with dense forests and among valleys and ravines. Picture it.: everything is pure mountains. There are very few flat areas. It seems like I'm back at Chacabulco. Yesterday we climbed one of the cliffs that Edward [her cousin] had thought could not be scaled. I held on very tightly to the horse's reins and began to go up very calmly, with the river flowing there below.[84]

Despite the enjoyment of her stay in Bucalemu, Juanita knew that her father had to be told of her decision to enter Carmel. Once back in Santiago at the end of March, she wrote a long letter to him, asking for his permission and explaining why she felt compelled towards Carmel. Letter 73 is a letter of great beauty, in which she bares her very soul, revealing things about her inner life she had shared with few others.

Juanita

Juanita described her search for true happiness, and how everything less than God failed to satisfy. In this context she rejects marriage which was not God's will personally for her. For Catholics, marriage is a sacrament which reflects the union between Jesus and His Church, and which therefore can bring married couples to great holiness; their mutual, life-long love is an image of Christ's love and flows from it; it is therefore a great sacrifice to offer to God:

> I wanted to be happy and searched for happiness everywhere. I dreamt of being very rich, but I saw that overnight rich people can become poor. [as happened in her own family]. And even if at times it doesn't happen, one sees that on the one hand riches abound, and on the other hand, people are overwhelmed by poverty of affection and unity. I've thought of happiness in the affection of a perfect young man, but the very idea that some day he might love me with less enthusiasm or that he could die, leaving me alone in the struggles of life, makes me reject the idea that by marrying I'll be happy.No. this doesn't satisfy me. For me, happiness is not found there. Where, then, I ask myself, is it to be found? Then I understood that I hadn't been born for earthly things but for eternal ones. Why go on denying this fact any longer? Only in God has my heart found its rest. With God my soul found itself fully satisfied, so that I desire nothing in this world but to belong to Him completely.
>
> …I understood that the world was too small for my immortal soul; and that only with the Infinite could my desires be satisfied, because the world and all that's in it is limited, whereas, by belonging to God, my soul would never tire of loving and contemplating Him, because in Him the horizons are infinite.
>
> … Don't think Daddy, that everything I'm telling you isn't breaking my heart to pieces. You know me well, and you know that I'm incapable of causing you any suffering on purpose. But even though my heart is bleeding, I must follow God's voice; it's necessary to leave the beings to which the soul finds itself intimately bound, in order to go and dwell with the God of love who knows how to reward the slightest sacrifice. How much more will He reward great sacrifice.[85]

Her father's unwillingness to face up to awkward situations had always distressed Juanita and especially so at this time. She needed his consent, and when he returned home shortly afterwards due to the birth of Chico and Lucia's baby girl, he had with him her letter. She spent two days trying to get him on his own, while he did his best to avoid her. When at last she met with him, he, in tears, gave his consent: 'If that's God's will, then I won't oppose it, since it will bring you happiness'. His tears cut Juanita to the quick: 'At that moment I felt the greatest pain of my life', she said, 'seeing that for the first time I was the cause of your tears'.[86]

She had her father's consent, and now she had to tell the rest of her family.

CHAPTER TEN

The Horizons Are Infinite

Her cousins, the Valdes Ossa girls, had invited Juanita and her father to spend a few days at their ranch in Cunaco. Her father decided not to go, so Juanita went on her own, spending a week with them for a much-needed rest. There, she sat down and wrote first to her father, thanking him for giving his consent, and then to Mother Angelica to say that her father had given her permission to enter, and the date was fixed for 7th May.

Now there was the burning question to answer: how to tell the rest of the family? This was solved when Luis inadvertently found Juanita's letter to her father, which he had left lying around. Perhaps not so inadvertently. Had Don Miguel left it lying where it would be found, saving him the difficult task of telling the rest of the family?

Luis was furious that other members of the family had been told and he himself left in the dark, since he was so close to his sister. Their father, to his credit, stood up for Juanita and her decision, saying, that knowing his daughter's strong will, to try and oppose her vocation would be like trying to stand in front of an avalanche. Juanita was still at Cunaco at the time, so she wrote a long letter to Luis, explaining at great depth and great beauty why she felt compelled to enter Carmel and of his rejection of religion:

My dear Luis,

Through my mother I heard that you're aware of my secret. Please forgive me for not having had the courage to confide it to you before. But I knew how much this news might disturb you and wanted to spare you as much as I could the pain you were going to feel when you became aware of everything …

> Can you hate religion of Jesus Christ, when it's religion and He who are granting me happiness in this life and in the next? What despair would have seized my heart when I discovered the emptiness, the nothingness of creatures, had I not known another Being capable of filling and satisfying me! No, I'd never believe that, Luis, of my soul, since I know that the religious beliefs in your soul are built on a solid foundation. And if this, unfortunately, should come to pass, I tell you that at this moment I'm entreating God that I might die myself instead, so that from my sacrifice light and love for our religion might be born in you.
>
> Furthermore, the One who placed in my soul the seed of my vocation was the Most Holy Virgin. And you were the one who taught me to love this tender Mother who's never been called upon in vain by her children. She loved me and finding no greater treasure to give me as proof of her singular protection for me, she gave me the blessed fruit of her womb, her Divine Son. What more could she have given me?[87]

Her family found it very hard to let go of such a loved and treasured daughter and sister. In the few weeks before her entry, her brothers were worried that Juanita wasn't going out to enjoy herself. Her mother was worried because she was wearing plain clothes, although Juanita said that she didn't like to appear poor to her friends and acquaintances. She persuaded her mother, who was the one most supportive of her, that there was no need to buy new clothes when she was so close to entering Carmel.

Shortly before her entrance, her mother loaned a Carmelite habit from the Santiago Carmel, and arranged for a professional photographer to photograph her. This was the custom of the time in Chile, that one entering an Order would be photographed in the habit beforehand. It is these photographs, together with the one of her in secular clothes, that are now so famous, and the only time she was to wear the black veil of final Profession.

The day before her entry she wrote to Miguel, who always remained close to her heart. During their years growing up she had sensed that he was deeply troubled, and which he expressed in his bohemian lifestyle. He might have thought that a nun would not understand a lifestyle so different from his, but Juanita assured him that she would always be with him. She gave him her crucifix, asking him, 'to wear it always as a remembrance of your sister:

> I understand, even though you never told me, that you're suffering, that you are a soul torn to pieces. Still, I often wanted to touch that wound, but your reserved character kept it from me. What could I do but be silent and pray for you? If you had known how much I wept for you, you would have listened to everything my soul wanted to tell you. But perhaps you didn't want to hear a nun's advice. Yes, I will be a nun, but I'll always have a sister's heart for you. I'll always keep watch over you from the convent and I'll accompany you everywhere with my poor prayers.[88]

If she showed a serene face to her family and friends, within Juanita was experiencing the darkest night she had ever had. Her yearning for Carmel, the joy that she had expected when the day had finally come, had dissipated, she felt a distaste for the step she was about to take, and only her unwavering desire to fulfil the will of God remained with her. As she stood before the door of Carmel in the anguish of the dark night of the soul, she nevertheless entered supremely prepared.

CHAPTER ELEVEN

I'm Happy

Juanita, entered the Carmel of Los Andes 7 May 1919.

There had been a storm the night before they travelled to the Carmel, which surely matched the heartbreak they were all going through, the last night of Juanita being with her family and the worry that the storm might have disrupted the trains. However, the storm passed, and the small group of family members took the train, after Juanita attended Mass with her mother.

As the doors of Carmel were ready to open to her, Juanita received the blessing of her mother and the Father Superior of the Carmelites of Santiago. Her father couldn't bear to be there. As she embraced Luis for the last time she whispered to him, 'God exists! Never forget that!' As for Rebecca, that day when they had giggled over trying on the postulant's dress was now gone. The distress she had had in school after Juanita left was a presage of her even greater distress now. Faced with the stark reality of losing her sister behind the forbidding enclosure doors she fainted.

As the cloister door closed behind her, Sr Teresa of Jesus knew that as she was entering the monastery her mission was to be a sister to everyone, the voice of prayer to God for everyone, especially the voice of those who did not know Him or refused to believe in Him, the voice for believers who wanted to draw closer to Him.

To be a sister in Carmel was a special title that had been proudly acknowledged from the very beginning of the Order, when the first monks named themselves 'the Brothers of Our Lady of Mount Carmel': Carmelites are the brothers and sisters of Our Lady. A Carmelite is a sign and a reminder to every baptised Christian, that, like them, they share spiritually in Our Lady's maternal role, bringing forth Christ in their own souls, and then bringing Him forth, also, spiritually by their prayer and sacrifices, in souls.

Sr Teresa of Jesus entered the large enclosure door, and as it closed behind her she kissed the large crucifix held out to her, and was then escorted to the Choir by her sisters singing 'O Gloriosa Virginum'. She stayed there in prayer for a short while then was embraced by her new family, saying with her voice and the radiance of her face, the darkness of soul now lifted, 'I am happy'.

She was then taken to her cell, which she described later to a friend:

> The walls are bare, and a wooden cross with a crown of thorns hang on one wall. The bed is wooden, with a straw mattress. While it's narrow, you can sleep very well there. We also have a little wooden table. It's very low. It's only a few inches up from the floor. At first it was almost impossible for me to write on the little table, sitting on the floor, but now I'm used to it.[89]

Before entering Carmel she had mused on the Carmelite life, painting it in her diary in the harshest of terms, especially about sitting on the floor: 'The Carmelite is poor. She possesses nothing. She must work to live. Her bed is a straw mattress. Her tunic is coarse. She doesn't even have a chair on' which to sit. Her food is rough and scarce.'[90]

This was true to a point but getting used to sitting on the floor and other customs had practical problems she hadn't foreseen!

The wooden cross bore the words of St Teresa of Avila, 'God alone suffices'; there was a little work basket and a wash basin in her cell, and that was all. There were other things to master, as well as sitting on the floor. Wearing her postulant's dress, there was so little time to dress once the rising bell had sounded that she arrived in Choir her first day with it all askew, her veil going in one direction and her cape another. She described it lightly to Rebecca, hoping that by giving her details of her new life she would lift her sister's distress:

In the morning I really have to work hard to get ready, since they give us only fifteen minutes. The first time I went out with my cape pulled to one side and with my veil to the other side, not knowing how to put it on; and everything else the same way. My Sisters helped me. The second day I pulled a trick; I woke up at five, got dressed to the underskirt and lay down. When they sounded the bell, I put on the rest of my things and was the first to go out to sing the wake-up greeting.[91]

I get into trouble at meal times, too, since the spoons are wooden, and the forks very small and narrow. It takes me a long time to eat and I have to do it after the others, but this is nice, since while my sisters are in the dining room, I stay in the choir with Our Lord, three quarters of an hour. I really enjoy it.[92]

On that first day, she also had to win the approval of a very important member of the ccommunity, Molzuc, a silver-coloured and very big dog. Mother Angelica gave Teresa a piece of bread to give to him, and a great friendship was sealed. 'The best part is that in the beginning, he's always fierce with everyone, but with me he's a big softie.' He might not have been so welcome a little later on, when he got into Teresa's cell and chewed up a notebook containing some retreat notes she had written. She had to send it to Rebecca with the request for her to rewrite it for her.

The parting had been heart-wrenching but Sr Teresa embraced her new life wholeheartedly; her letters and diary reflect her joy while, right from the start, that joy was founded on her embracing a life of sacrifice. She also had promptings from the Lord, urging her to the greatest observance of the Rule and customs, an obedience to His slightest will:

14 May 1919. I'm now in Carmel 8 days. Eight days of heaven. I feel divine love in such a way that there are moments when I believe

I'm unable to endure it. I want to be a pure host and continually sacrifice myself for priests and sinners. I made my sacrifice without tears. What strength God gave me in those moments. How I felt my heart torn to pieces on hearing the sighs of my brothers and sisters. But I held on to God and that was enough.

Our Lord reproaches me for my minor imperfections and asks the smallest sacrifices, but it's inconceivable how much they cost me. He asked me to live in continual recollection and to look to no-one. And I'm to do everything out of love. I should obey at the slightest indication and have a great spirit of faith.[93]

Rebecca felt the pain of separation so much that she continued to have fainting fits at the very thought of her sister in Carmel. The separation was no less keen for Teresa, not only knowing how badly Rebecca was reacting to losing her, as well as the pain of her whole family, as she described 20th May:

At night I felt an immense pain of separation. I was imagining Rebecca alone in our room and crying. I ardently desired to hug and embrace each of the ones I left for Jesus. I didn't know the pain I was going through and whether I should tell our dear Mother Superior, since it seemed to me that I was seeking consolation from a creature. But I told Our Lord that if she comes in to leave us in the novitiate, I'll tell her; otherwise, I'll be silent. But Our Lord, as usual, spoiled me, and, contrary to our custom, permitted her to come. I told her my sorrow and she took me to the choir where I began to tremble because of the violence of the pain. Thanks to the prayers of our dear Mother I remained more in peace and was able to sleep afterward.[94]

She received a letter from Luis, who was still unable to understand the step his beloved sister had taken. Sometimes, when Luis had expressed his doubts to her, she would rest her head against him and say, 'Don't you sense God when you're with me?' Teresa tried to instil in him some of the fire of love which was burning within her:

> Dear Luis, despite the distance separating us, my soul will always be one with yours. We both form but a single soul, isn't that so? Well, then, I've already been gathered up to God. His love is my soul's life. I want to bring you up there to Him; I want to share with you, my dear brother, a little of the fire in which I am set aflame; I want to warm you with that infinite warmth, so that you may have life. I ask only that you have good will. Allow me, my Luis, to be your guide.[95]

Teresa was assigned to work in the garden, a task she had never done before. 'What a wreck I'll probably make!' she wrote to her sister. 'I wish you could get some little carnations from my aunt Teresa to plant, because there are very few here. The other day I went with Rev. Mother to trim the rose bushes.'[96]

Later, she wrote to her father about her success as a gardener, seeing here an interest they could share together:

> Many times, when I'm working in our garden, I think about Chacabuco, San Javier, and I feel happy as I work. The other day they had me planting the vegetables. May God watch over them that they not be lost. But you can really see how Providence is with us since we have vegetables and fruits in abundance. Everything is of the best quality.
>
> And your crops, how are they doing? Tell me everything. You know already that everything that concerns you is of interest to me. I'd love to see you freed of all those sad thoughts and filled with peace.[97]

It was helpful to her to be able to share such things in her new life that would be of interest to her family, so they could see how simple their life was; it was helpful for them to know that she was so happy and settled her monastery and that they could help in small ways. She was soon asking Rebecca for other items and more plants as the community prepared little gifts for the Prioress's feast-day:

> Please buy me thread and the things I need to make little woven baskets: glue, brown paint, and tell me how to glue them because I've forgotten how. Also, I wish you'd make me a little model, or send me the little gilded basket. But I need it soon because it is for Rev. Mother's feast day. Also, I'd be grateful if you'd send me some plaster to make those medallions and explain how they're made. And send the holy cards I left, that is, the pictures of saints. Even if there's writing on them, it doesn't matter ...
>
> When Mom sends me the roses and carnations, I hope you can get me some of those white flowers that have such a lovely scent and look like jasmine. And send me the Persian violets, because we have a very pretty oratory with a statue of the Most Holy Virgin and a cute little Child Jesus. I hope you can get a little song book with hymns to the Sacred Heart from the Sisters, because here we have only a few hymns. Later I'll send you that music I got at school, too. Forgive me for asking so many favours but you won't mind. Send me that little note book soon.[98]

Once she had become familiar with the Carmelite day, she described it to Rebecca. The Sisters rose at 5.15, and had an hour of prayer from 6 o'clock, followed by praying the Divine Office and Mass. At 9 o'clock they go to the Novitiate to receive the necessary permission from the Prioress to write letters, etc. followed by a breakfast in a little side room: 'We put our cups on little benches and sit on the floor'. This was probably for the postulants only, to introduce them gradually into the life. This was followed by work – sweeping, sewing in her cell. At the main meal in the refectory the novices have soup made from meat, again, to bridge the gap gradually to the meatless Carmelite diet: 'We have soup made from meat (the novices) and a dish made from green beans, very plentiful, like Uncle Pancho used to make, and there is fruit and a cup of tea with milk'.[99] There were two sisters in the Novitiate with her, she aaid, Sr Teresa Eugenia de la Eucarista and Sr Isabel de la Trinidad.

She also helped with the washing up, again, something she had never done before: 'After the meal, at 12.15, I must go to wash the dishes (only this week). The first day I did it by myself I forgot to put the cover on the washbasins and the water began to spill out. I don't know what would have happened had it not been for a very kind little extern sister who came to my rescue.'[100]

Recreation followed the meal and then there was free time until 2 o'clock when Vespers was prayed, followed by spiritual reading. There was then work and devotions until an hour of prayer from 5 to 6, followed by supper and recreation, and lights out at 11 o'clock. During the recreation period, the sisters would often sing, accompanied on the guitar and bandurias, a type of stringed instrument.

When she was in her cell she would be sewing; 'Since we are poor, we mend and darn our clothes over and over again. Imagine one habit having more than one hundred and fifty patches.' It was not unusual for a habit to have so many patches that in the end there was none of the original cloth left! 'Right now I'm stitching a purificator,' she added in a letter to her friend Maria Ramirez. 'I don't know how many mistakes I'll make. But you already know how I am.'[101]

She was delighted when she was given the task of ringing the rising bell, which meant she had a little extra time to herself in choir, and she was soon trying her hand at cooking. Her joy in her new life spilled over, as she wrote to her friend Elisa Ossa, her words, as so often, echoing those of St Elizabeth of the Trinity: 'I'm the happiest creature in the world. I'm beginning my life of heaven, of adoration, and unending love. it seems to me as if I'm already in eternity, because you don't feel time here at Carmel. We're immersed in the bosom of the Unchanging God.'[102]

The Divine Office was an unexpected revelation. The Divine Office, the official Prayer of the Church, is an obligation on all priests and religious, and is increasingly popular with lay people also, who often pray the Morning, Evening and Night prayer from it.

'During the Divine Office I imagine that I'm in heaven', Teresa wrote to Rebecca, 'It's also the most precious time of all.' The Divine Office was said or sung in Latin in the monastery, but as she had learnt Latin at school, that wasn't a problem for her. The first time she had to recite a lesson solo in the middle of the Choir, as most postulants discover, is for some reason a daunting event, and the tradition in the Los Andes Carmel was to have a little celebration for them afterwards:

> Can you imagine that they had me read the lesson in Latin at morning prayer? You can imagine how scared I was. I was almost in tears (as always) and first I got totally confused about everything I was to do and say; and since I couldn't speak, I had to write to Sister Pedagogue (who's the one who teaches us what we're to do). You can't imagine how upset I was ... the Sub-Prioress, who's in charge of the choir, gave me a present (they always do that), since it was the first time I'd read. She came to the Novitiate with a tray of fruits, chocolate, brown sugar candy and cookies; and my Sister novices and I delighted over it all with our Rev. Mother and Mother Sub-Prioress.[103]

Once she had mastered the intricacies of the Divine Office it became a joy to her and she soon delved into the depths of its richness. She described it in some detail to an unnamed friend, who was thinking of entering Carmel herself:

> I want to speak to you about the Divine Office. You know that it is the Church's ceaseless cry lifted up to God. We, contemplatives, are entrusted with crying out on behalf of the world. When we are in choir we are like the angels praising God; we form part of

that angelic concert; and our antiphons are stanzas of that pure, divine poetry. Don't we become then the angels who sing before the Tabernacle to console Jesus in His sad prison? Jesus, too, sings with His Carmelites. He raises up, together with His brides, that pure supplicant cry for the world to His eternal Father.[104]

In August, to her delight, she was put in charge of the Novitiate sacristy. She had to arrange the oratory there and take care of the whole novitiate. That same month, the community celebrated the Silver Jubilee of Sr Mary of St Joseph, the community's infirmarian. Teresa had written to her mother, asking her to send her six nickel teaspoons and a nickel statue of the Holy Family, which she could give to the sister:

> You can't imagine how much we celebrated her feast day. So much so that the poor little thing, in her humility – for she is a saint – began to cry. There were funny poems, songs on the guitar, etc. We enjoyed ourselves so very much. In Carmel everything is simplicity and joy, and everyone tries to do all she can to make her Sisters happy. It's really delightful to live amidst such holy Sisters, for they form one heart.[105]

In every community there will be differences in character and personality, and it was no different in the Los Andes Carmel. Mother Angelica said that Sr Liusa de la Santissimo Sacramento, Sister Pedagogue, the Sister who helped her in training the novices, noticed nothing exceptional in Teresa; she was probably the sister whom Teresa described as being 'a thorn in her side' as she picked up on every little fault she noticed in her. Another Sister refused, after her death, to see that she was a saint, saying that according to her, Teresa didn't have a true Carmelite vocation and seemed 'too full of herself'. But they were few who did not love and appreciate her. When it came to voting whether to admit her to being clothed with the longed-for Carmelite habit, the community was unanimous, and in a letter to her mother, 10th September, Teresa announced the good news:

> I have some very good news for you: on the feast of Mary's Nativity, [8th September], our Rev. Mother proposed me to the chapter to decide whether I may receive the habit of the Order. And I obtained all the necessary votes from my Sisters. You can't imagine my surprise and emotion, for I had no idea that when she called me to the room, it was because the vote had already been taken. I entered the room trembling. The whole community was assembled, and our Rev Mother was presiding in her white choir mantle. Believe me, I thought I had been rejected. When I heard her tell me that I'd been accepted, I don't know what came over me. And our Rev. Mother immediately embraced me, an embrace that lasted a long time, since I didn't let her go, as I couldn't imagine how to thank her. Then I began to hug them all – I almost disarmed them – so much that they teased me about it later. Truly, only God can repay them for accepting me, since besides being so bad I'm useless.[106]

Her mother also received the Carmelite habit as a Third Order Carmelite at the end of September, taking the name of Sr Maria Magdalena and beating her daughter to it, as Teresa said with some envy. Teresa was clothed in the habit on the feast of St Teresa of Avila, her namesake, 15th October.

After her Clothing and as a Novice Teresa was expected to follow the Rule in its fulness. In a letter to her mother she commented on gossip in Santiago that had got back to the Carmel saying that she was sad, weeping. She did weep, but not from sadness at being in Carmel. She wept at not feeling she loved Our Lord enough; she wept as she united herself to his Passion; as to being sad:

> I'm still laughing at all that our Rev Mother told me is being said in the world about this poor Carmelite. Mommy, why do they want

I'm Happy

to upset you, telling you that I am sad, that I weep, etc? Why does the world try to awaken the dead for its own sake, finding sadness in those who live in Jesus' arms? Can't they see that it's envy of the repose and of the peace and happiness flooding my soul? How clearly I see that those who invent these kinds of lies don't know what it's like to live in Carmel and what such a vocation really implies! Besides, if in my letters, Mommy, you notice joy and happiness, how can they believe that I'm so duplicitous as to express precisely the opposite of what I feel?

Right now I look at my Jesus and laugh with Him at the whole world. Let me weep in His arms all day long, while the rest laugh and amuse themselves; how little I mind weeping, gazing upon infinite joy and tasting bitterness with the divine sweetness of my Jesus. I'm happy and I shall never cease to be so, for I belong to my God. In Him I find my heaven, my eternal, unchanging love. I want nothing but Him. I love no one more than Him. And this love continues to grow in my soul to the extent that I'm brought into His divine Heart of love and adorable perfections.[107]

Some of her family came to visit her, but not her father, however much she pleaded with him. She wrote to him just before Lent, said that she hadn't received a reply to her last letter, although she had received news of other members of her family:

I'm so happy that Miguel is with you, as he will be company for you, and this will be good for him. Tell him he's done a fine job on his promise of writing to me, and that I hadn't thought he'd be so ungrateful to his own sister, whom he knows perfectly well loves him so much. I've heard nothing about your harvest or about that business he told me about in his last letter.

You can't imagine, Daddy dear, how much I pray for you each day, and at night. I always say a Hail Mary to the Most Holy Virgin asking her to protect and keep you company, since your Carmelite daughter can only do that by her thoughts. Mommy sent me some pictures of Lucetita and Ignacito. I really enjoyed them. Believe me, I was amazed at how chubby the little baby is. It seems like they are having a good time at the beach Are you going to Algorrobo for a little swimming? I beg you to go, even if it's for only eight days.[108]

It was a good idea for Miguel to help his father on the farm. His mother was at her wits end with his drinking, even going so far as to say it might be better if he died. Perhaps she was praying that the open air and hard work would help him to recover.

Teresa had hoped her father would come and visit her in the New Year, but this was not to be, and then Lent began. At her First Holy Communion, Juanita had asked the Lord that she might die, such was her happiness on that day. Since then, she had had an intimation that she would die young, which was why she wanted to know from her spiritual director which was the quickest way, Carmel or the Sacred Heart Sisters, to become holy. During the first days of Lent, in March, she told Fr Avertano, the monastery chaplain, that she would die within a month. She followed all the austerities of Lent and Holy Week. On Holy Thursday, 1st April, she spent almost the whole day in choir until 1 o'clock in the morning.

The following day, at noon on Good Friday, she recited the Way of the Cross with the community in the choir and took part in the Three Hours Devotion and other chants, then remained kneeling before the Cross for some time. Later, in the Novitiate, the Novice Mistress felt an urge to knock on Teresa's cell door and noticed that her face was very inflamed and red. Finding that she had a temperature and a high fever, the Novice Mistress sent her to bed.

When the doctor came to see her and asked how long she had felt ill, Teresa said she had felt unwell for a month, but had tried her best to hide it. The doctor diagnosed typhus, at that time almost incurable. None of the remedies he gave her helped at all, and on Easter Monday she asked to go to confession and received Holy Communion. She also received Holy Communion the following day, but in the night she had a convulsion; the priest was called again and gave her the anointing of the sick, Extreme Unction, which then was only given when there was danger of death.

Teresa revived around 12.30 at night and asked to make her vows, which she made with great joy. She received Holy Communion the next morning, her last, because from then on the typhus took hold very rapidly. She was in great pain, so much so that even a sip of water was agony for her. Almost in a coma from the pain she yet obeyed instantly to take medicine if the sister said it was Mother Angelica's will for her, saying 'the victim of love must climb to calvary'.

Her family, of course, was informed and her mother came, hoping, without success, to obtain special permission to enter the monastery to see her. Teresa was too ill to be taken to the speak-room to see her mother, but at least she was nearby. The last letter she wrote was to her mother, the last words she wrote were to assure her mother that 'her Mother and Sisters were showering her with love and attentions'.[109]

Teresa of Jesus of the Andes slipped peacefully away to God 12th April, 7.15 a.m., surrounded by the sisters who loved her so much.

She was taken down to the choir an hour later, while the sisters kept vigil by her side during the night. 'She did not lose her angelic beauty and appeared to be sleeping, said Mother Angelica. On the death of a sister a circular letter is sent round to all the Carmels in the country, describing their life and asking for prayer. In the letter Mother Angelica wrote she summed up the impression that Teresa had made on her sisters during her short stay in their midst; she gave an account of Teresa's short life, summing up at the end:

> The deep impression of the sanctity of our angelic Sister, Teresa of Jesus, remains with us. These thoughts are based on having seen her practice virtue in the form already described and her manner of being by which her most pure soul was revealed...
>
> We watched her pass as a ray of light, like a vision, and her absence has left a most profound sorrow in our hearts but we have

thanked the Lord for having drawn her to our Monastery and for having permitted us to contemplate sanctity in such a young girl.[110]

I'm Happy

'*Juanita seated (left) with friends in Algorrobo*'.

Juanita

PART TWO

My Ideal, Jesus, My Infinite Ideal

Introduction

Shortly before she entered Carmel, Juanita wrote in her diary that she would soon consign its pages to the fire. Fortunately, this did not happen, because her family persuaded her to keep it and Fr Blanch agreed with them. She took it into Carmel with her, so she wrote in it events that happened there also. It is unlikely that Mother Ríos, to whom it was dedicated, ever saw it.

Her diary, together with the 164 extant letters she wrote to friends, family, her spiritual directors and Mother Angelica, are an indispensable resource for following Juanita, Saint Teresa of Jesus of Los Andes, on her journey to exceptional holiness and union with God. They also add to the priceless wealth of mystical writings within the Catholic Church. They show the young Juanita valiantly responding to Our Lord's call to follow Him.

She was the near contemporary of two other young Carmelite saints, Thérèse of the Child Jesus and Elizabeth of the Trinity. Their spiritual writings influenced Juanita's own spiritual life, and our three young saints – who all died young - form a trinity of Carmelite spirituality that has had, and continues to have, great popularity and influence on countless souls striving for union with God, both Catholic and non-Catholic.

Saint Thérèse of the Child Jesus gave to the Church her 'Little Way' of trust and surrender to the good God. Saint Elizabeth of the Trinity taught souls to enter into an inner silence and find within their own souls the Most Holy Trinity, the divine indwelling. What is the distinctive charism, what is message that Saint Teresa of Los Andes was chosen to give to us?

There is, first of all, the appeal she has for young people, who flock in thousands to her shrine every year. They see in her 'one of us', someone who enjoyed sports, living in a loving but sometimes troubled family, with a wide circle of friends, who enjoyed holidays with them, yet within that ordinary framework she lived in close union with the love of her life, Jesus Christ. They can relate to that; young people are idealistic, they want challenges and something to aim for. Teresa can lead them to see what inspired her, what was the great ideal, her 'Infinite Ideal', Jesus Christ, to whom she gave her life. She offers them a challenge, to give their lives to Someone who will never let them down, but who warns them that following Him has a cost.

To choose to follow Jesus is not an easy option, and Teresa showed how costly it can be. But she then showed that, as Jesus Himself promised, they will find a pearl of great price, something that is worth giving up everything to obtain, and the joy, the infinite joy that it brings and that never tarnishes.

This is a message for everyone, not just for young people. Having followed Teresa's life, among her family, at school, on holiday, we now dig deeper into her spiritual life, and the path and the means that brought her to such great sanctity that the Church has raised her to the altars as an exemplar and a model for others to follow. It is a message for us, so I will draw out the lessons that we can learn from her in our own spiritual journey.

The writings of Saint John of the Cross and Saint Teresa of Avila are the masters to turn to in understanding a soul's journey to God, especially in the light of the Carmelite charism and which we find so admirably illustrated in Teresa of Los Andes' life. Even more than in the lives of Thérèse and Elizabeth, the spiritual path mapped out by John of the Cross and Teresa of Avila, is even clearer, as our young saint goes from the foothills of Mount Carmel, or the outer courts of the Interior Castle, to the heights of the mystical marriage of union with God, providing a living example of what they were writing about.

My Ideal, Jesus, My Infinite Ideal

As we examine her life, this may seem somewhat strange, because, unlike Thérèse and Elizabeth, Teresa's life was filled with exceptional charisms that few are privileged to experience. St Teresa of Avila beautifully called them 'favours'. We will look at what these experiences meant for her and find in our own lives that Jesus gives us graces, too, not necessarily so exceptional, but exactly what we, individually, need to follow Jesus wholeheartedly.

Teresa the Mystic

Teresa of Los Andes was a mystic. There are mystics in every religion and none, but Catholic mysticism has a specific characteristic. The Catechism of the Catholic Church, describes mystical union thus:

> 2014 Spiritual progress tends towards ever more intimate union with Christ. This union is called 'mystical' because it participates in the mystery of Christ through the sacraments. – 'the holy mysteries' – and, in him, in the mystery of the Holy Trinity, God calls us all to this intimate union with him, even if the special graces or extraordinary signs of this mystical life are granted only to some for the sake of manifesting the gratuitous gift given to all.
>
> 2015 The way of perfection passes by way of the Cross. There is no holiness without renunciation and spiritual battle. Spiritual progress entails the ascesis and mortification that gradually lead to living in the peace and joy of the Beatitudes.

The Catechism is saying here that every Catholic is a mystic when they participate in the mystery of Christ present in the sacraments, and especially in the holiest of mysteries, the life of the Holy Trinity. God gives extraordinary signs to some in order to remind us of the free gift of grace God offers to all. By giving Juanita special graces He intended them to be a reminder to us, to show us what immense gifts we are being given, just as she was, even though we so often receive them 'as through a glass darkly'. The penetrating eye of a soul totally given to God lifts the veil somewhat, inviting us to penetrate these mysteries with them, to deepen our understanding of them, and so increase our love for them. Then they can work in us, too, that marvel of transformation in Christ Jesus that was worked in Juanita.

To live the mystical life doesn't necessarily include 'extraordinary signs': St Thérèse of Lisieux and St Elizabeth of the Trinity, two of the foremost mystics of modern times, were graced with few *extraordinary* mystical gifts. St Teresa of Jesus of Los Andes, on the other hand, received them throughout her life. According to the Catechism, all those who partake of the mysteries are mystics, that is, if we allow the sacraments to really take root in our lives, then they will open up to us the life of God Himself, as the life of the Most Holy Trinity, dwelling within us penetrates and transforms us. The Catholic mystical life flows through and from Jesus Christ, not from anything a person can strive to obtain for himself.

The Catechism says that the mystical life always goes by way of the cross, and there is no avoiding it. Rather, by following in the footsteps of Jesus, suffering is embraced, self-giving and renunciation is united to His suffering and leads to a peace and joy, even in the midst of suffering, that the world cannot give.

In raising a person to the altars, to beatify and canonize them, the Church does not take into account extraordinary experiences; rather, she looks at how a person responds to them with greater humility, love and surrender to God's will. The Church says that Teresa showed such characteristics to that heroic degree within an ordinary life and in circumstances that can happen to anyone.

Teresa lived in Carmel for only eleven months, so her journey of holiness was lived for the most part 'in the world'. In Carmel, God perfected and refined all that had gone before in her life to bring it to the perfection of Spiritual Union. This is the journey we will follow now.

In this second part of my book, I will be drawing on the writings of St John of the Cross and St Teresa of Avila, and also on those of St Thérèse of Lisieux and St Elizabeth of the Trinity, to place St Teresa of Los Andes in her rightful place as another mystic and spiritual guide within the Carmelite tradition.

To avoid confusion, I will use the name of Juanita, even when drawing on events from her time in Carmel and her writings from that period.

CHAPTER ONE
Caught In The Nets Of The Divine Fisherman

With her expansive nature, Juanita loved the wide-open spaces, the ocean, the night sky of her native land; they all spoke to her of God and His immensity, an immensity of love. It was on such a night that she sat with Luis under the stars, when he told her that to him they were cold and impersonal, making him feel alone in a pitiless universe. He remembered how Juanita would sing in her beautiful voice while contemplating the stars:

> Those were unforgettable dialogues, he recalled. I would ask, 'Don't you feel terror before the infinite spaces, like Pascal used to say?' Juanita answered me, 'Why feel fear? Isn't it God's house? Far from scaring me, the infinite spaces accompany and move me so that my soul wants to fly through them with the trust of a child of God.' She was so used to the infinity of God, in which she so loved to immerse herself, that the beauty of earth was but a small reflection of the grandeur of God, which was her natural and familiar home.[111]

Luis saw God only as a philosophical construct and could feel no love towards Him. Juanita knew God only in the warmth of the Father, knowing His Spirit in her heart and the love of Jesus coming to her in the Eucharist and at every moment. In the Sacred Humanity of Jesus she found everything she could desire. In the words of St John of the Cross:

> If I had already told you all things in My Word, My Son, and if I had no other word, what answer or revelation can I now make that would surpass this? Fasten your eyes on Him alone, because in Him I have spoken and revealed all, and in Him you shall discover even more than you ask for or desire. [112]

Juanita could gaze at the boundless heavens and not feel crushed by their greatness. Her God was infinitely greater than His creation, and she could lose herself in the infinity of God, knowing from experience His love, brought to her in the humanity of Jesus; that He comes as brother, spouse and lover to His children whom He loves with an infinite love:

> Tell me, is there anything good, beautiful or true that we can imagine that is not there in Jesus, not in a superior way now, but infinitely? Wisdom, in which nothing is secret; a power, for which nothing is impossible (the sphere in which it operates is nothingness); a truth, which excludes absolutely everything that is not (He Himself said 'I AM THE ONE WHO AM'), justice, which led Him to become man in order to take away sin and disorder of men; a providence which never stops pardoning; a goodness that makes Him forget His creatures' offences; a love which contains within itself all the tenderness of a mother, a brother, a spouse, making Him leave the bounds of His greatness and links Him closely with His creatures; a beauty, that is ecstasy…? What other thing imaginable is there in the depth of the soul that is not found infinitely there in the God-Man? [113]

Meditating on Jesus' birth at Bethlehem and Mary's contemplation of Him, she wrote:

> She sees that little Child, crying in the arms of His poor Mother, and those tears are the ones of the One who is infinite Joy. How

can we fail to love that Jesus with our whole soul? He, who is uncreated Beauty, He, Wisdom eternal, He, Goodness, Life and Love. how can our soul fail to be inflamed with charity at the sight of that God dragged through the streets of Jerusalem with His cross on His shoulders; at the sight of that God becoming food for His creatures, transforming Himself in bread in order to be one with them, to divinize and convert them into Himself? Oh, love Jesus. Who can ever return your love better? He thirsts for your heart. Don't you feel that when after receiving Communion He says to you: 'Daughter, give me your heart'?[114]

Her friend, Carmen Ortuzar, also wished to become a Carmelite, and Juanita described to her the infinite horizons in Carmel, that were opening her up even more to the love of Jesus Christ, her Lord:

> If you but knew how we come upon discovering infinite horizons never known before. If you could only live, my sister, a Carmelite's life of intimate union with Jesus … He is everything to her. How many hours does she spend in choir by the grilles, contemplating His uncreated Beauty, listening to the infinite Wisdom Jesus teaches her and, above all, experiencing the heartbeat of her God? Nothing can separate her from Him. Jesus has taken her from the world, from her loved ones, to bring her to the solitude where He takes His rest, that He might have her to be His host.[115]

In the important letter she wrote to her sister Rebecca describing her vocation to Carmel, Juanita introduces us to the foundation of her spiritual journey. She describes herself as 'caught in the nets of the Divine Fisherman.' She is telling us that she has become as fascinated and drawn to love the person of Jesus Christ no less intimately than those first disciples in the Gospels. It is a person-to-person relationship with the Man Jesus, who leads us, through His humanity, to the inner depths of the Most Holy Trinity.

Religion, the manifestations of it, can become outward observance, but for a Christian, Scripture reading, the sacraments, the liturgy, the prayers, the life of the Church, have but one purpose: they are there to bring us to a closer relationship with God. Indeed, in the sacraments, especially, Jesus Christ Himself is present, giving Himself to us beneath the outward forms.

There is an incident in the life of St Thérèse of Lisieux, that illustrates that even someone in the religious life may not have experienced that personal relationship God desires to have with us. Sr Madeleine, one of her novices, was with her in her room one day:

> Thérèse suddenly 'said to me in a tone of voice that I cannot reproduce: "God is not loved enough! And yet He is so good and so kind... Oh how I wish I could die!" And then she began to sob. Not understanding what it was to love God so vehemently, I looked on in amazement, and wondered what kind of extraordinary creature I was standing in front of'.[116]

It was this sort of love that Thérèse had and that Juanita possessed from her earliest years; to which all the practices of our Christian life should tend.

This intense love of Jesus Christ was at the heart of Juanita's spirituality, nourished by her deep prayer life, drawing her into an ever-closer union with Him. 'It seems to me that I have found my Heaven on earth, since Heaven is God and God is in my soul', said St Elizabeth of the Trinity[117] and Juanita made this totally her own, too, as she explained to her friend Elena Gonzales:

> I feel Him so intimately united to me, that I want nothing more, except the beatific vision in heaven. I feel I'm filled with God, and then I hold Him close to my heart and ask Him to make me experience the perfections of His love. There's no separation between us. Wherever I go, God is with me in my poor heart.

> That's the little house where I dwell; it's my heaven here on earth. I live with God; and despite being on walks, we converse with each other without anyone being able to surprise us or interrupt us.[118]

In this long letter to Elena Juanita was able to share her inner life with her friend because they both shared the same secret, a call to the religious life, Elena to the Sacred Heart Sisters, Juanita to Carmel. In the letter she describes a common problem: how can one love someone whom one cannot see or hug – something that was so important to Juanita in her love for her family. But God, made visible in Jesus, has made it possible for us to have some touches of the Divine, says Juanita, because He knows that our human nature needs them. In the sacraments He uses water at our baptism, oil at our Confirmation, then, supremely in the Eucharist, He comes to us in a form we can touch and see. This is the importance of the image and reality of the Sacred Heart, which was one of the pillars of her spiritual life. In picture form it represents the immense, burning love He has for us.

'For me, heaven is begun and always in progress', said St Elizabeth of the Trinity and for Juanita, too, her divine guest in her soul was heaven on earth:

> Tell me, is there anything greater on earth than the eternal, immutable, all-powerful God searching out a soul on earth to make her His bride and seeking a human heart to join to His own Divine Heart, and in love achieving the most complete fusion? Further yet, that God would come down to earth and live here in the Eucharist, dying of love for us? Think of the greatest love on earth, and what is it in comparison with the love of an Infinite God? ...
>
> Believe me. I'm speaking to you sincerely: I used to believe it was impossible ever to fall in love with a God who is unseen, with someone who can't be hugged and touched. But today I can affirm with my hand over my heart that God completely makes up for

that sacrifice. You feel that love so much and those caresses from Our Lord, that it seems that God is there by your side. I feel Him so intimately united to me, that I want nothing more, except the beatific vision in heaven.[119]

In the letter she wrote to her sister Rebecca describing her call to Carmel, she reveals there, too, her ardent love for Jesus:

I've given myself over to Him. On the 8th of December I promised myself to Him. It's impossible to say how much I love Him. My mind is filled with Him alone. He is my ideal, my infinite ideal ... I wish I could set you afire with that love. how happy I would be if I could give you to Him! Oh, I never need anything, because in Jesus I find everything I'm searching for! He never leaves me. His love never diminishes. He's so pure, so beautiful, he is goodness itself.[120]

The Sacred Heart

There are various themes in Juanita's spiritual life that developed more strongly in Carmel; one of these is her love of the Sacred Heart, which the Sisters at her school would have taught her. The Sacred Heart is a devotion much loved of Catholics, who usually have a representation of It in their homes. The Sacred Heart reveals the human love in the Heart of Jesus, which is at the same time divine love. In depictions of the Sacred Heart, the Heart of Jesus is pierced, crowned with thorns and blazing with the fire of love. This depiction shows, firstly, a Heart wounded by humans through their indifference and even hatred; it is a Heart that blazes with love for everyone, a blazing love that, as Juanita prays, will burn up everything imperfect in her and then burn her up in the flames of Divine Love of union with God. It is a Heart that seeks for and longs for, other souls whom he wills to set ablaze with that same love. It became the focus of Juanita's love for God; she saw the Sacred Heart in the Host she received in Holy Communion and the two are inseparably intertwined.

Not long after her entry into Carmel the community entered the month of June dedicated to the Sacred Heart. 'Today marks eight days since I died to the world in order to live hidden in the Infinite Heart of Jesus', she writes 14th May to Elisa Ossa and to Hermania Ossa she writes:

> I'm the happiest person alive. I lack for nothing because my whole being is satiated with the love of God. how I wish, little sister of mine, that every one of my letters might bring you a little spark of divine love! How happy I'd be if I could make you fall in love with my Jesus. This Friday ask the Sacred Heart of Jesus to make you love Him and be His friend. What a treasury you'll find in that Divine Heart! Day and night He's knocking at your heart's door, asking you for a little spot there, for a little love. Won't you open up to Him, offering Him your warmth? He's calling to you from the tabernacle. From out of all eternity, He's been wanting you to receive Him in Communion every day. He's a God who doesn't need you and, yet, who died for love of you. and won't you go to free Him from His prison, where He's locked up for your sake?[121]

> Enter into His Divine Heart, where I live submerged, breathing only on the divine, and consuming my many miseries in the fire of His love. That's where I live, contemplating the grandeur of His Divinity. First I look at God – that incomparable Trinity – plunging myself into the bosom of my Father, of my Spouse, of my Sanctifier; and then I look at the eternal Word made flesh, at my Divine Jesus. That's when I sing my praise of glory and of love. [122]

> I've just come from the choir where I spent an hour within His

Heart. An hour lost in the Fountain of Love. how delightful is the life I'm living![123]

And I ask myself why the Lord protects and keeps me for Himself when I'm so miserable? And it is in Jesus Himself that I find my answer. He has a heart of God, filled, then, with infinite love, and this fire of love consumes everything that it finds in its path, as long as we let ourselves be consumed. Rev. Mother, ask the Divine Heart of Jesus to devour me in the flames of His love, and that He may consume there all my miseries and imperfections so I'll be more faithful to Him each day and arrive at complete union with Him.[124]

To Graciela Larrain she wrote:

Please help me to be good. Tell me what you plan to do during the month of the Sacred Heart. Let's ask our dear Jesus what He desires of us. Let's consecrate ourselves to Him. Let's give Him our heart, our freedom and all we have. Our Lord really likes to dwell in our soul. Let's offer it so that He may live there.[125]

To all her friends, to everyone, Juanita had the same longing: to set others afire with the love that was burning within her.

CHAPTER TWO

The Goal Of Prayer Is To Kindle In Us The Love Of Our God

It is unsurprising that her close friends, and those who shared her desire for the religious life, should seek her advice on prayer, sensing her own deep prayer life. Her friend, Elena Gonzalez, asked her advice about prayer, and Juanita began with the basics. As always, her prayer is directed to the sacred humanity of Jesus, nourished by the Eucharist, with Our Lady guiding her always to her Son:

> Meditation consists of looking at Our Lord the way He was here on earth, of seeing how He prayed, and of working to make ourselves like to Him. There's another kind of prayer I find to be more simple: speaking with Our Lord as one speaks with a friend, asking for His advice, promising never to offend Him, telling Him you love Him, etc., Set aside a time for prayer; set aside ten or fifteen minutes, whatever you like. But always imagine Our Lord there in your soul and do the same when you go to Communion. You can also share your little home with the Most Holy Virgin. You can tell her all your secrets and ask her to keep you wholly for Jesus.[126]

In her forthright way, St Teresa of Avila was adamant that no matter how advanced in prayer a person was, they should never abandon the sacred humanity of Jesus, of thinking about the saints, as some who were advanced in prayer were saying to her:

> I cannot imagine what such souls are thinking of. To be always withdrawn from corporeal things and enkindled in love is the trait of angelic spirits not of those who live in mortal bodies. It's necessary that we speak to, think about, and become the companions of those who having had a mortal body accomplished such great feats for God. how much more is it necessary not to withdraw through one's own efforts from all our good and help which is the most sacred humanity of our Lord Jesus Christ.[127]

As Our Lord told her, when she was complaining that she couldn't remain recollected while working in the kitchen: 'Teresa, you're not in heaven yet!'

While she was in San Pablo, Juanita had the same problem. Her days were so filled with activity, no church was open for Mass so she couldn't receive Holy Communion and felt she was unable to pray; but because her whole life was oriented to God and to His will, then she was in a state of continual prayer, as she described to Mother Angelica:

> Many times, dear Mother, I can't even pray. This is my greatest pain, because I'm constantly in the company of others, and they never leave me alone even for one moment. Yesterday I got discouraged, but Our Lord consoled me by telling me that I should force myself to control such sadness and discouragement, since I'll have to be in control of myself often in the face of difficulties in order to become a holy Carmelite. That alone was enough to encourage me and made me very happy with God's will. I'm grateful to Him.
>
> It's true that sometimes I don't get to pray, but my life – I can say - is a constant prayer. Everything I do, I do out of love for my Jesus…[128]

Joy in Prayer

In a letter to her friend Inés Pereira Juanita encourages her friend in the joy that comes from prayer, drawing her closer to Jesus:

> If you give yourself to prayer, you'll find that God will show Himself to you, and make you fall in love with Him. In prayer our soul seeks Him out, and if we do so, wanting to know and love Him, Jesus will raise a bit the veil that conceals Him and show us His divine Face, radiant with beauty and sweetness. There are times when He will open His Heart's wound, and will show us the treasures of His infinite goodness and love. At other times He lets His sweet voice be heard, leaving the soul consumed by love and repentance.[129]

Wordless Prayer

In wordless prayer people are happy just with being with the Lord. This can turn into a silent gazing on God that God Himself initiates into the prayer of quiet. St Elizabeth of the Trinity herself relates that a sister came to her to say that she felt her prayer had too many words Elizabeth replied by saying that her prayer had too few.

Writing to Elisa Ossa, Juanita recognized that not everyone finds discursive prayer, prayer using the imagination, to their taste. Some are drawn to this wordless prayer, who are happy to just 'be' before the Lord. This is different from the prayer of quiet, where it is God Himself who draws the soul to a prayer of just 'being' and the soul finds that she can no longer meditate with the imagination, or use vocal prayer.

> Don't be discouraged if you can't make discursive prayer or don't know what to say to Our Lord. He's well aware of how

miserable we are. Who would know what to say to the Word, the eternal Word, the divine and uncreated Wisdom? The same thing has happened to me many times and I don't think my prayer is bad because of it, because the goal of prayer is to kindle in us the love of our God. when we're there in His presence, if just gazing on Him is enough to make us love Him, and if we are captivated by His Beauty that we can't say anything but that we love Him, why, little sister, should we be upset? Our Holy Mother recommends this loving gazing at our soul's Spouse.[130]

Juanita loved to imagine herself, like Mary, sitting at the feet of Jesus, simply talking to Him, but, more importantly, listening to Him. Her spiritual directors encouraged her in meditative prayer, and she gave an example of this:

> I meditated on the Prayer in the Garden. Our Lord drew me close to Himself. I saw His dying face. I felt He was cold. He prayed for me to His Father so that at least I wouldn't abandon Him and that I would remain faithful. I felt fervour but pain for having offended Him.[131]

In 1917, Juanita felt that she needed more spiritual direction, and her mother recommended her own spiritual director, Fr José Blanch, a Claretian Father, who guided her skilfully and wisely until her death. As he was sometimes away from Santiago, through the letters she wrote to him and which he kept, he has left us a rich legacy of Juanita's spiritual journey. He asked her about her prayer, and in a diary entry for April 1917, she said she told him 'there were periods when I was unable to meditate, and I remained tranquil with Our Lord. He said I must always strive to reflect, and to do the other only as a last resort'.[132]

This transition from meditative to contemplative prayer is a very delicate one to discern, and St John of the Cross gives helpful advice on it (Ascent. Bk 11, Ch. 13 - 15). That Fr Blanch recommended that she continue with discursive prayer perhaps means that perhaps he hadn't yet discerned that God was already drawing the young, 16-year-old Juanita to the higher form of prayer.

St John of the Cross says there are three signs that a soul is being drawn to the Prayer of Quiet: not to receive satisfaction from discursive meditation, a disinclination to fix the imagination on particular objects, a liking to remain alone in loving awareness of God, without particular considerations. 'Meditation must only be discontinued when the soul is placed in that peace and quietude' of the third sign. The person gradually transitions from one to the other, but:

> When the spiritual person cannot meditate, he should learn to remain in God's presence with a loving attention and a tranquil intellect, even though he seems to himself to be idle. For, little by little and very soon the divine calm and peace with a wondrous, sublime knowledge of God, enveloped in divine love, will be infused into his soul.[133]

'Prayer of Quiet'

Juanita's prayer was often 'the prayer of quiet', which she described as 'I experience an ardent desire to contemplate God, but it seems that my understanding finds itself immersed in a darkness that impedes contemplation.'[134]

If at this time Juanita was enjoying the prayer of quiet, then according to St John of the Cross she should not force herself to try to meditate. When beginning the practice of prayer it is helpful to use the imagination to think about a passage in the Gospels, for example, in the way described by St Ignatius in his *Spiritual Exercises*. At some point however, the Lord may wish to take us a little further:

> [I]n this doctrine it will be opportune to point out in this chapter [13] when one ought to discontinue discursive meditation so that the practice will not be abandoned sooner or later than required by the spirit. Just as it is fit to abandon it at the proper time that it may not be a hindrance in the journey to God, it is also necessary not to abandon this imaginative meditation before the due time so that there be no regression.[135]

St John of the Cross goes on to describe the prayer of quiet as loving knowledge, peace, calm, almost imperceptible at first:

> But the more habituated he becomes to this calm, the deeper his experience of the general, loving knowledge of God will grow. This knowledge is more enjoyable than all other things, because without the soul's labour it affords peace, rest, savour and delight.[136]

This doesn't mean that one never returns to meditative prayer, but to be happy when drawn into a quiet 'being' with God and returning to meditative prayer when it feels right. Juanita describes one such example of the prayer of quiet:

> The love I feel is not sensible, but much more interior. In prayer there are things happening that never happened before: I remain completely steeped in God. I can't make reflective prayer. It's as though I'm sleeping in God. In this way I experience His greatness and so great is the joy I'm experiencing in my soul as something coming from God. it seems to me that I find I'm completely immersed in the divinity.[137]

Darkness of soul

Juanita's prayer was not, of course, always one of consolations and delight, and she went through necessary periods of darkness of soul, dryness in prayer, which is normal for anyone taking seriously the life of prayer, prayer which includes intercession and a determination to do God's will:

> Lord, if it please You that the darkness of my soul becomes deeper, that I not see You, it will not bother me because I want to fulfil Your will. I want to spend my life in suffering to make reparation for sins, those of sinners and so that priests will be sanctified. I don't want to be happy, but I want You to be happy. I want to be like a soldier so that at every moment you can dispose of my will and preferences. I want to be courageous, strong and generous in serving You, Lord. You are the Spouse of my soul.[138]

In her first letter to Fr José Blanch, Juanita described her state of soul at that time (the beginning of April 1918), which was one of dryness and abandonment. An interesting point to note in this extract is that 'the tempest abated', but her aridity continued. Aridity and dryness in prayer can stem from various sources: perhaps there is some fault within oneself that we have not acknowledged or sought to amend. But sometimes it is from Our Lord, who takes us into the desert so that we can be purified of selfishness, perhaps, seeking the consolations of God rather than the God of consolations. It is a test of love if we persevere, even when we don't think we are getting anything out of our prayer.

There is another, deeper reason, and that is that Our Lord is drawing us into the redemptive sharing in His own abandonment on the cross and His darkness of soul whenHe cried out, 'My God, my God, why have You abandoned Me?'(cf Matthew 27:46). Juanita took strength from the fact that although she felt abandoned by the Lord, at a far deeper level she knew He was always there with her:

I've suffered so much dryness and abandonment, that it's impossible to describe. Especially because I once spent a whole hour and a half in such terrible straits, that I said to myself, if this continues I'll be unable to do anything. I felt such solitude and complete abandonment. At the same time, I saw that I had no one with whom I could discuss all this. And that caused me great suffering. I asked Our Lord to remove that anguish, and then He let me hear His voice, and immediately, at His word, the tempest abated; although I continued to experience aridity. But this doesn't surprise me, Rev. Father, since I was the one who asked Christ to deprive me of all consolation, that other souls I love may encounter peace and joy in the sacraments and in prayer.[139]

Locutions

At the time of her First Communion Juanita received the first sound of her Saviour's voice:

It is impossible to describe what took place between my soul and Jesus. I asked him a thousand times that he would take me, and I experienced his dear voice for the first time. Oh Jesus I love you. I adore you! I prayed to him for everybody. And I felt the Virgin near me. Oh, how my heart expanded! For the first time I experienced a delicious peace.[140]

She went into more detail of that experience in a letter addressed to a Jesuit priest Fr Antonio Falgueras:

Since I was about seven years old, there was a very great devotion born in my soul to my Mother, the Most Holy Virgin. I told her everything that happened to me and she spoke to me. I heard her voice clearly and distinctly in my soul. She advised me and told me what I must do to please Our Lord. I thought that this was something natural, and it never occurred to me to speak of what the Most Holy Virgin was telling me.

From the time of my First Communion, Our Lord spoke to me after Communion and told me things that were going to happen, and then they really did occur. But I went on thinking that everybody who went to Communion was treated this way.[141]

As we have seen, Juanita realised that these locutions of Our Lord were not something that happened to everyone only when a remark she made to her mother made her realise otherwise. From then on, she was very reticent about them. In reading her letters, she never writes of them to her friends and family, but only to the priests who were guiding her. She always sought the advice of her directors in everything she did and the experiences she received, giving her confidence that she was on the right path and humility that Our Lord should come to such a 'criminal nothingness as herself.

Later in the letter to Fr Falgueras she says that 'what Our Lord requested for my sanctification, the priest [her confessor] would later repeat with the same words in the confessional'.

Test All Things

There was an incident that occurred when Juanita was very young, but already spiritually attuned to the things of the spirit. It is a reminder that with all spiritual charisms, it is important to 'test all things', because the devil can appear as an angel of light (which he once was), and we have to be firmly rooted in humility and the things of God to discern what is true and what is not. It is likely that Juanita was asking about things concerning the Faith. Our Lady can only respond with truth, which, as Juanita said, gave her certainty, rooting her more firmly in the Faith. The devil can only lie and disturb us, make us uncertain concerning the things of God. If a charism is from God it brings peace:

> My devotion to the Virgin was very great. One day when I was very troubled by something, I told this to the Virgin and asked Her for the conversion of a sinner. Then She answered me. After that, when I called her the Virgin spoke to me. Once, I asked her about a doubt I had. Then, a voice answered me. I said to it: 'That is not the voice of my Mother, because she can't be telling me this'. I called her and she said that the devil had answered me. I became fearful. Then she told me that whenever I heard the voice I should ask: 'Are you my Mother?' And this is what I always do. Every time I wanted to know something I asked Her and what She told me gave me certainty.[142]

As Juanita shows, it isn't wrong to have doubts, because to question the Faith in a genuine desire to understand more deeply will encourage us to explore the truths of our faith and bring us to a greater understanding and therefore growth and spiritual maturity.

As she progressed in the spiritual life her locutions became fewer, and she learnt not to ask Our Lord anything just for her own curiosity, as well as being careful about whether a locution came from God or not:

> Our Lord would speak with me but much less. And now He never tells me anything that is not for my soul alone, since once I began to ask Him about many things which had nothing to do with my soul. Then He told me not to question Him, but to be content with what He told me. Only twice did He tell me things that didn't happen. That's why I don't think it was Our Lord who said them to me. Still, His words always leave me with peace, humility, repentance and recollection.[143]

What are locutions?

Juanita received locutions in which she said she heard Our Lord, and sometimes Our Lady, speaking to her, giving her guidance. In the Scriptures we are told many times that 'the Lord said to me' and there are various ways in which God can communicate Himself to us.]

St John of the Cross discusses locutions in The Ascent of Mount Carmel, Book 11, Chapters 28-31. His description of what he calls 'successive locutions' seems to best fit the type of locution that Juanita normally received:

> Successive words always occur when the spirit is recollected and attentively absorbed in some consideration. A person will reason about his subject, proceeding thought by thought, forming precise words and judgments, deducing and discovering such unknown truths, with so much ease and clarity, that it will seem to him he is doing nothing and that another person is interiorly reasoning, answering and teaching him.
>
> Indeed, there is every reason for this belief, since he reasons with himself and replies as of carrying on a dialogue. In a way he really is speaking with another for, though he reasons with his intellect as the instrument, the Holy Spirit frequently helps him to form these true concepts, words and judgments, and thus he utters them to himself as though to another person. Since his intellect is recollected and united with the truth, which is the subject of his thought, and the Holy Spirit is also united with him in that truth, - for He is every truth – it results that, while his intellect is communing with the divine Spirit by means of that truth, it simultaneously forms interiorly and successively the other truths about its subject, while the Holy Spirit, the Teacher, leads the way and gives light.[144]

In other words, it was the voice of the Holy Spirit, who is the Spirit of both the Father and the Son, which Juanita received as 'the sweet voice' of Jesus. It seems that in some way she distinguished between receiving instruction from Our Lord that was received in an auditory way in her soul and this interior understanding. To Fr Cea, a priest she met in San |Pablo, she describes one time when she received messages from Our Lord in a non-auditory way, as an interior understanding:

> The other day He talked to me about poverty, telling me that I should try to possess neither my own will nor judgment, because for the time being I really can't be poor. Then He told me that I should be attached to nothing. But all this was done wordlessly, because He made me understand all these things interiorly, and also made me realise that I was attached to sensible feelings of fervour. He made me understand that I'd been making divine union consist of a sensitive love, but that I was to imitate His divine perfections, becoming more and more like Him, and suffering greatly for love of Him, being crucified like Him.[145]

Juanita herself gave her definition, her understanding of locutions, which would correspond to St John of the Cross's successive locutions':

> However, there is another kind of prayer, and it is called a locution. This consists in interiorly experiencing a voice that seems to be, now Our Lord or the Most Holy Virgin, telling us what we should do to be good, or to do something else. Sometimes it is our own understanding itself rapidly reading things; at other times, it is Our Lord inspiring us. Nevertheless, the only thing we should pay attention to is the good received from that communication without trying to figure out whether it comes from God or from our own reason.[146]

St John of the Cross describes another form of locution which he calls 'substantial locutions':

> Although these locutions are also formal, since they are impressed very formally in the soul, they nevertheless are different in that their effect is vital and substantial ... only the word that impresses its significance substantially upon the soul. For example, if our Lord should say substantially to the soul: 'Be good,' it would immediately be substantially good; or if He should say: 'Love Me,' it would at once have and experience within itself the substance of the love of God.[147]

Juanita spoke from her own experience from hearing such locutions. In her very first locution of hearing 'His sweet voice' she also experienced peace, one of the primary proofs that a locution is genuine. As an example of a 'substantial location' she heard Our Lord saying to her; 'my dear friend', which would have embedded deep within her soul the truth that she was indeed His dear friend. In John 15:14 Jesus says to His disciples: 'You are my friends if you do what I command you'. In obeying His commands, in making her life correspond to that of her Lord, Juanita was becoming His dear friend, something that Jesus says to every disciple who does likewise:

> But in the meantime, the years I'll have to wait before I give Him the most sweet name of Spouse seems like centuries. How sad are the days of this exile! Yet He's united to me and very often says to me: 'my dearest friend.' This infuses strength into me and I go on forcing myself to make myself a little less unworthy of the title that I'll bear.[148]

> Our Lord took pity on me and allowed me to hear His voice in my heart. Then it was all over and I was filled with peace.[149]

[F]rom the depths of the tabernacle He said to me, 'I want you to become a Carmelite'. Peace returned then to my soul.[150]

Such examples are a reminder that God can speak to us in many ways, especially through the Scriptures: it could be a word of love, assurance, guidance or warning; it can be received when a word or phrase of Scripture, which we might have read many times before, or a truth of the faith, suddenly leaps out with new meaning. It can be something in spiritual reading, something said in a sermon, or by a friend, a quiet interior voice which may advise us to do one thing or another, guiding us. It is sometimes just one word, such as 'peace', or a phrase, 'do not be afraid', that is perceived with such power that it immediately takes effect in the soul.

Juanita said that when it is the Lord who speaks to her 'His words always leave me with peace, humility, repentance and recollection'. In this way she could discern whether it was truly Our Lord speaking and not another spirit; receiving a word from another spirit happened a couple of times, which left her disturbed, and what it said did not come to pass, a sure sign that the words did not come from God, as she herself recognised.

CHAPTER THREE
Apostle Of The Eucharist
Jesus Is My Nourishment

During her sickness when she was fourteen years old Our Lord began to open up to Juanita the mysteries of the Sacred Host in the tabernacle. She heard the voice of Our Lord, saying, 'What! I, Juanita, am alone on the altar for love of you and you can't even suffer one moment of solitude?'[151] 'Jesus made me understand', she added, 'how abandoned and lonely He is in the tabernacle. He told me to keep Him company'.

Juanita had accompanied her mother and her aunt to daily Mass from the age of six, and after her First Holy Communion received Our Lord daily when it was at all possible. This exchange began a journey that brought Juanita into the depths of understanding, not only of the Mass, of receiving Holy Communion, but also the worship and reverence for the Sacred Host reserved in the tabernacle. The Mass was at the centre of her life because that is where she found Jesus, bringing her to the most intense union with Him. For her and in truth, Jesus is just as present in the Host as He was when He walked the paths of Palestine:

> Love Him greatly, but get to know Him. It is in the Eucharist that Jesus is present; that God who wept, who sighed and suffered our miseries. That bread contains a divine heart with the tenderness of a shepherd, a father, a mother, and a spouse, and God. let's listen to Him, for He is Truth. Let's gaze upon Him, for He is the image of the Father. Let's love Him, for He is the love Who gives Himself for His creatures. He comes to our souls that they may be lost, deified, in Him. What union, however great it may be, can be

compared with this one? And I eat Jesus. He is my nourishment. I am assimilated by Him. What greater happiness is there than this: to hold tightly in our heart, the God who is our God![152]

Each day Jesus nourishes me with His adorable Body and, together with this delicate food, I hear a sweet and soft voice like the harmonious echoes of the angels of heaven. This is the voice that guides me, that loosens the sails of the ship of my soul so I will not perish, will not sink. I always hear that dear voice which is the voice of my Beloved, the voice of Jesus, in the depths of my soul. And in my pains, in my temptations, He is my Consoler, He is my Captain.[153]

St Teresa of Avila also had the same message:

One day, one of the sisters said to St Teresa of Avila, 'I wish that I had lived at the time of Jesus Christ, my dear Saviour, for then I could have seen how amiable and loving He is'. St Teresa, hearing this laughed. 'What! Do you not know then, dear sister, that the same Jesus Christ is still with us on earth, that He lives quite near us, in our churches, on our altars, in the Blessed Sacrament?'[154]

Preparing for Communion

Juanita encouraged her friends to go to daily Mass and Communion, as we see in her correspondence with Herminia Ossa. Herminia says that she doesn't experience the happiness that Juanita feels when going to Holy Communion, and in response Juanita asked her how she prepared for it:

> To me, it's inconceivable that, yearning for happiness, you don't search for Jesus. After Communion we have everything. We have Him whole and entire, because we have God who is our heaven in this exile. You will tell me that you feel nothing of this happiness. But I ask you: how have you prepared for it? Have you delved into God's grandeur, into the infinite love He demonstrates by reducing Himself to a host? When you go to Communion, reflect on what you are about to do: receive a completely eternal Being who doesn't need you, since He is all-powerful, an immense Being who is everywhere, an infinite and majestic Being before whom the angels with their purity tremble. He comes, filled with infinite love for you, a poor creature full of sin and misery. Among the many people of the world, you are honoured with a visit by that great King. Still more, that you may draw near to receive Him, He casts aside His splendour, and under the form of bread, the simplest form of nourishment, He unites Himself to His poor creature and makes Himself one with her. And while He is afire with infinite love, she remains cold and indifferent and shows no gratitude for so signal a favour.[155]

Juanita realised that it was vital to prepare before going to Mass. She meditated, in her prayer pondered on the greatness of God, which threw into stark contrast for her the infinite grandeur of God who yet takes the humblest of material things to come to us as our food and drink. The reception of Our Lord in Holy Communion brings us to a closeness of union with Him that exceeds anything else and is our entry into heaven on earth, yet we often receive Him thinking only of ourselves. Jesus comes to us, to 'every believing soul', not only to give Himself, but to receive from us 'comfort and love'; just as Jesus was made welcome in the home of his friends Mary, Martha and Lazarus, so Jesus wants to come and make His home within us:

> For a Carmelite, Communion is heaven; and Communion should be the same for every believing soul. Why don't we die of love in seeing that God found it far too little to give us His infinite love

drop by drop. In His infinite love He wants to give us more, and yet humanity prepares His death. He becomes our food in order to give us life. A God who is nourishment, bread for His creatures, isn't that enough to make us die of love? And to think that we receive Communion without the least spark of love! Jesus comes full of infinite love, and we receive Him coldly concerned only with seeking favours for ourselves, without adoring Him, without weeping our gratitude at His divine feet. He comes in search of comfort and love, finding nothing.[156]

May your every Communion be better, since Communion is the life of our soul. Pray to Him for everyone, because He will refuse you nothing, and later, throughout the day, hug Him often close to your heart and continue giving Him your thanks, yearning for your next Communion. This is a moment of heaven during our earthly exile. Let us long for Him.[157]

Preparing for Mass

In a letter to two of the family's well-loved servants Juanita advises them how to prepare for receiving Holy Communion: Having received Our Lord at Mass, He should then accompany us throughout the day. We may not recognise the growth in us that this brings, but that growth will be there, just as earthly food and drink nourishes the well-being of our bodies:

I'd also really like to hear that you go to Communion every day. Communion is heaven on earth for the soul who truly understands what she is doing. Reflect carefully that it is Jesus who's coming to you. That Jesus is God, the Creator of everything we see, the All Powerful One. Remember that He has no need of you, since He is Master of all things, but despite being the Holy One, He makes Himself one with you, even though you have offended

Him so often. He comes filled with infinite love, to unite Himself completely to you, and after having made you good, He will lead you one day to heaven. How good is our Jesus, who loves us so much! Let's love Jesus and show Him our love by receiving Him every day. Let's free Him from His cold prison and shelter Him in our hearts, so poor, yet filled with love.[158]

There are various ways of preparing ourselves for the joy of being at Mass, joining with the priest in uniting ourselves with the offering Jesus makes to His Father, then receiving Our Lord in Holy Communion: we observe the eucharistic fast, perhaps reading the readings of the Mass beforehand, trying to remain prayerful and staying in prayer in church before Mass and thanksgiving afterwards. It is helpful to read books about the Mass to deepen our understanding and appreciation of it.

Juanita, like Herminia, sometimes felt dryness when going to Holy Communion, so could understand how she felt; nevertheless she continued to go, regardless of her feelings. Since Christ Himself had given us such a gift of Himself, had commanded us to do this in remembrance of Him, then regardless of whether we feel fervour or not, He wants our will to do His will. Then He will work wonders in the depths of our soul beyond thought or feeling:

> I experience only horrible dryness in my prayer. It's of such a nature that I find myself immersed in darkness, and it's impossible for me to keep my thoughts on God nor can I recollect myself. When I go to Communion, I don't feel a thing. I'm like a stone with Our Lord, so much so, Rev. Father, that desires come to me of not wanting to receive Communion because of the evil I do.[159]

As she related to Fr Blanch, 'My normal state of soul of one of terrible dryness. I'm often distracted at Communion time. I don't feel the least bit of fervour in my heart. Still, even though I don't feel drawn to it in any way, I haven't stopped going to Communion'.[160] She was learning to go beyond feelings, because her faith was still there, as she says to Mother Angelica:

> I'll get up early to pray for an hour, Mother, for me that hour is sometimes a heaven; but at other times there's so much darkness in my soul that I can't discover my Jesus there. Throughout this year, except for a few days, my prayer and Communion have been like that; so much, in fact, that at times, I don't feel like going to Communion, because I say to myself: what, do you think Jesus wants you going to receive Him in Communion with your soul as hard as a rock? Still, a love not felt that lives in the deepest part of my soul makes me go up to receive Jesus.[161]

Graces Received

Juanita also received great graces when praying before the Blessed Sacrament. The locution she received and accepted led her to receiving an intellectual vision of Our Lord, which did not come from her own imagination, as she was unable to construct it afterwards from her own imagination:

> Another time I was very fervently and humbly praying in the presence of the Blessed Sacrament. He told me then that He would like me to have a more intimate life with Him. He said I must suffer a lot, as well as other things that I don't remember. Since that time I've been more recollected, and I saw Our Lord very clearly praying as if I'd seen a picture of Him. But I didn't see Him with my body's eyes, but just as He showed Himself to me. It was very vivid, and even though at times I wanted to represent Him this way, I've been unable to do so. I saw Him that way, I think, for more than eight days, but later I didn't see Him any more. And now I can't do it, either.[162]

This was perhaps the time during her holiday in Algorrobo when she went into the chapel to pray one afternoon during the siesta when most people would be resting. One of the mission fathers, Fr Felix Henlé, went into the chapel and found Juanita in ecstasy. Her eyes were fixed on the tabernacle, her hands clasped in prayer, her face burning and radiant; she was levitating some 30 centimetres from the ground. Fr Henlé left the chapel in silence, greatly moved.[163]

Mystical Union

It was in Carmel that her mystical union, nourished by Our Lord in the Sacred Host, deepened. Juanita describes an experience she received before the Blessed Sacrament. The letter was to Fr Cea, and in it she asks him to remember her when he offers Mass. To offer ourselves up to God at the consecration at Mass is a profound way for God to give us the grace we need to be saints:

> About a year ago, though, I think it was one day when the Blessed Sacrament was exposed, Our Lord revealed Himself to me with infinite love. At that time He made me understand how people fail to respond to His love. then He asked me to offer myself up as a victim of love and expiation and assured me that I would suffer greatly in my life …
>
> And I repeat again: God will repay you for all your prayers, especially for your great kindness in remembering me at the consecration of the Mass. I assure you that it made me happy, since I was really longing for a priest to offer me up and bathe me in that divine Blood. But I believe that by the strength of so many prayers, God will complete in me the work of my sanctification. By God's grace, I will be a saint.[164]

Juanita was brought more and more into amazement and awe that the eternal God should humble Himself to become bread for us. Only the God of Love in love with humanity could conceive of such a thing:

> I was trying to do things when all of a sudden the thought of God's humbling Himself under the form of bread came to my mind. So much love was given me that I couldn't resist it, and with awesome strength my soul was being drawn to God. Afterward I felt a sweetness inundating me with peace. That convinced me that it was God.[165]

Just before she left school Juanita made a retreat and wrote down notes of the subjects covered. Under the heading 'The Last Supper' she wrote a meditation on the Eucharist which gives a description of the great reverence and profound love she had for the Eucharist and also the wonder of Jesus' humility in coming to us under the appearance of bread and wine:

> When they speak of the Eucharist I feel something strange in myself that I'm unable to think or do anything. It's as though I'm paralyzed and I believe that if in that instant there came to me impulses of love I'd be unable to resist them. My Jesus, I annihilate myself before Your love! You, God of heaven and earth, of the seas, of the mountains, of the star studded firmament, You, Lord, who are adored by the angels in an ecstasy of love; You, Jesus in Your humanity; You, the living bread! Oh, to be annihilated, all this would be so little! If they had left a relic of You it would be a token of love worthy of our veneration; but You Yourself remain, knowing that You would be the object of profanations, sacrileges, ungratefulness, abandonment. Lord, are you mad with love? You are not just in one place on earth for us but in all the tabernacles throughout the world. Oh, Lord, how good You are, how great is Your love that You make it appear to be nothing. What is more, You disappear by letting them see a creature, a criminal nothingness.[166]

Prisoner of the Tabernacle

'Every Sunday we have the Blessed Sacrament exposed in the oratory,' wrote St Elizabeth of the Trinity. 'When I open the door and contemplate the divine Prisoner who has made me a prisoner in this dear Carmel, it seems to me rather like the gate of Heaven opening!'[167]

This was a thought that Juanita made her own. In the Carmelite life many hours a day are spent in Choir, close to the Tabernacle: at Mass, praying the Divine Office, the hours of silent prayer. The grilles that separate the Choir from the Sanctuary only emphasise the impression of being a prisoner – but the Carmelite is also a prisoner of mutual love, just as everyone is who spends time in prayer before the tabernacle:

> What is more beautiful to a loving soul than to spend her life by the Tabernacle! He, a prisoner of her love, and she a prisoner of His. Nothing separates them. There is no other occupation. They are only to love one another, the creature losing herself in His infinite Goodness. He opens His Heart to her, and there makes her live oblivious to all worldly things, for He reveals to her His infinite charm, before which all else is vanity. He embraces and unites her to Himself. And the soul, lost and overcome with love amid the tenderness of one who is God Himself, despises created things, wanting only to live with Love alone.[168]

She spoke of Jesus alone in the 'cold' tabernacle and loved to visit a church and pray before the tabernacle. But even when we can't visit a church in person and pray there for a while, just as we can make a spiritual communion, so we can make a spiritual visit to Our Lord in the tabernacle at any time. Juanita shared this thought, a quotation, with her sister Rebecca, but didn't know the source:

A Tabernacle has the silence of a tomb, the majesty of a throne, the delights of life. And it's because the tabernacle contains Jesus as an immolated victim, as King of the world, as the nourishment of the soul.[169]

A host through the Host

To her friend Elisa she wrote a beautiful meditation on the Host as a pattern for their own lives:

Jesus is a host on the altar. He hides Himself. A host, apparently does not see or hear, or speak, or complain …In the same way, if we ourselves want to be hosts, we must hide from the gaze of others…

A host has no will of her own. To obey without answering back and to obey even what seems contrary to our own judgement, to be silent for God…

The Sacred Host is in a little ciborium. We, as hosts, should seek poverty, choosing the least appealing things for ourselves, without others noticing it…

The Sacred Host is pure. We should flee from the affection of every creature. Our heart is for Him alone, it belongs only to Him…

The Sacred Host is given to human beings. We should give ourselves entirely, or better still, offer ourselves – for it's not suitable to be given – to everyone around us. This will make us charitable, but always seeing Jesus in our neighbour.[170]

In a diary entry, Juanita takes this image of the host to even greater extremes in relation to herself:

May 22. In prayer Our Lord showed me how He was ground and converted into a host for us. He told me that to be a host it's necessary to die to self. A host – a Carmelite – must crucify her thoughts by rejecting all that's not of God. She must have her thoughts always fixed on God, her desires directed to the glory of God and to the sanctification of her soul. A host doesn't have a will of her own as to where she is to be taken. A host doesn't see or hear, doesn't communicate exteriorly, but only interiorly.[171]

She repeats this image in a letter to Fr Blanch, adding another dimension, that this dying to self and allowing herself to become a pure host, is so that other souls may possess that same love. This is one of the most profound aspects of the Communion of Saints, that in Christ we are united one to another, so that one person's prayer and self-denial and love of God can affect others and draw them closer to God; and, of course, the opposite is also true. This puts a great responsibility on one's shoulders, both for good or ill:

I hunger to receive Him in Communion, but He doesn't reveal Himself to me. Still, I recognise that I deserve all this because of my sins, and I want to suffer. I want Jesus to grind me to flour within that I may become a pure host where He can take His rest. I want to be athirst for love that other souls may possess the love which this poor Carmelite yearns for.[172]

In a mirror image of Jesus being offered to the Father on the altar at Mass, Juanita sees herself as being offered likewise to the Father:

Jesus wants her to be His host, Jesus lives in her and sacrifices her upon His Heart, silently offering her to His Eternal Father for a sinful world, while He – having become a host – secretly immolates Himself on the altar.[173]

> Offer up your Carmelite at least once as a host at your holy Mass. I want to be a host through the Mass. I want to be a host through the Host. Place me in the chalice that, bathed in the Blood of Jesus, I may be accepted by the Most Holy Trinity.[174]

In the letter to Amelia Montes she delves even deeper into the union of the soul, not just that of a Carmelite, who becomes by extension another Christ bringing Him to souls as He comes to us in the sacrifice of the Mass:

> He has made me like unto Himself by transforming me into a host. Yes, a Carmelite is a host who carries Jesus within herself. She is not the one acting. It is He. He sacrifices her, offers her in silence, just as He sacrifices and immolates Himself silently on the altar. She prays always with Jesus at the altar; she saves souls but by looking to Jesus. She sheds her heart's blood by denying herself in all things. She has sacrificed everything for Jesus.[175]

Ecstasy of Love

For Juanita, receiving Communion brought her into the most intense union with God, in wonder that the great God could come to dwell in her nothingness:

> If we prepared ourselves each morning a little better to receive Communion, how we would spend the entire day in an ecstasy of love with that immense, majestic God, become food for our souls! In heaven, my little sister, the angels contemplate Him face to face, but we human beings, each of us possess Him and can identify ourselves with Him. At those moments when my soul is

united with God, everything else ceases for me. Words fail me, my little sister, they fail to express the divine happiness I feel. I experience the Infinite One, the Eternal, the all-powerful Holy One and the God of Wisdom joined with my poor emptiness. Then I adore and love Him more. This is when the soul feels pure. It is in the fountain of holiness.[176]

> After I receive Communion, I feel as if I'm in heaven dominated by the infinite love of my God. Sometimes my only consolation in this exile is holy Communion, where I unite myself with Him without fear of losing Him through sin. This desire makes me flee from the slightest imperfections since they separate me from the One who is infinitely holy.[177]

Juanita focussed mostly on the individual's reception of Communion, but when she went on pilgrimage to the Lourdes grotto in Chile in February 1917 she gained an insight into the universal nature of the Church, that at Mass we are united to the liturgy of heaven; the saints and angels are worshipping; Mary is there, too, offering the people's prayers to her Son, and every believer is united as one body in the Communion of Saints:

> Yes, my Mother. At Lourdes I found heaven. God was on the altar surrounded by angels and you, from the concave of the rock, offered Him the cries of the multitude kneeling before your altar. You asked Him to hear the supplications of the people banished in this valley of tears, while at the same time, together with their hymns, they were offering you their hearts full of love and gratitude.[178]

CHAPTER FOUR
I Really Love The Most Holy Virgin

Our Lady was with Teresa throughout her life, guiding her always towards her Son. Teresa made a promise to Luis at the time of her First Communion that she would say the rosary every day and remembered only one occasion when she forgot to do so. As she wrote to her father:

> From the time I was a little girl, I really loved the Most Holy Virgin, to whom I confided all my dealings. Only to her did I unburden myself, and I never underwent a joy that I didn't reveal to her. She responded to that love. She protected me and listened to everything I asked her. And she taught me to love Our Lord. She placed the seed of a vocation in my soul.[179]

After that visit to the Lourdes Shrine in Santiago 10th and 11 February 1917, Juanita composed the following prayer. It is astounding that this beautiful prayer to Our Lady was written by Juanita when she was only 16 years old:

> Yes, Mother, you are the celestial Madonna who guides us. You allow heavenly rays to fall from your maternal hands. I didn't believe such happiness could exist on earth; yesterday my heart, while thirsting for it, found it. My soul was ecstatic at your virginal feet, listening to you. You were speaking and your maternal language was so tender. It was from heaven, almost divine.
>
> In seeing you so pure, so tender, and so compassionate, who would not be encouraged to unburden his intimate sufferings to

you? Who would not ask you to be his star on this stormy sea? Who is there who would not cry in your arms without instantly receiving your immaculate kisses of love and comfort? If he be a sinner, your caresses will soften him. If one of your devoted ones, your presence would enkindle the living flame of divine love. If he be poor, you with your powerful hand will aid him and show him the homeland. If rich, you will sustain him with your breath against the dangers of his very agitated life. If one is in affliction, you with your tearful gaze will show him the cross and on it your Divine Son. Who will not find balm for his pains by considering the torments of Jesus and Mary? The sick man finds in your maternal heart the water of salvation that allows your enchanting smile to blossom forth, and makes him smile with love and happiness. Yes, Mary, you are Mother of the entire universe. Your heart is filled with sweetness. At your feet let the priest prostrate himself with the same confidence as the virgin in order to find in your arms the fullness of your love. The rich as well as the poor will find in your heart their heaven. The afflicted as well as the happy can find on your mouth a celestial smile. The sick as well as the healthy can find caresses from your sweet hand. And finally, sinners like myself find in you a protecting Mother who can crush beneath her immaculate feet the head of the dragon. And in your eyes I see mercy, pardon and a shining lamp to keep me free from falling into the muddy waters of sin.[180]

I'm Alone, My Mother

Juanita instinctively turned to Our Lady for help in conquering herself, and her prayer for peace of heart was answered.

When she again felt overwhelmed with everything, when Ignacio hurt his leg badly, she wrote a very moving letter to Our Lady, asking for her help. It illustrates how tender was her love for Our Lady. The prayer turns, of course, to Jesus, as Mary leads her to her Son.

She came across this letter a while later, and included it in her diary, when she was again going through a rough patch. When talking of Dark Nights, this is not confined only to prayer, but often includes external circumstances surrounding us. Juanita is in pain, but she gives it a spiritual dimension in offering it to Jesus, by taking a little bit of His Cross from Him:

> Dear Mother, Mother I almost idolize you. I write to you to unburden my heart that is being torn apart by pain. I do not wish, Mother of my soul, that you join its pieces but that my heart distil a little blood. The pain is choking me, my Mother. I'm suffering, but I'm happy suffering. I've taken the Cross from my Jesus. He is resting. What greater happiness could I have?
>
> I'm alone, my Mother. My mama is going to visit Viña today to see little Ignacio and will remain here. How long? I don't know. As long as Jesus wants. How does that seem so to you? I suffer ... and I can do no more. I only ask that you heal the sick. You know who they are. You, Mother, can do this if you wish. My Mother, show that you are my Mother. Listen to the cry of my sinful but repentant soul, that suffers and consumes the chalice of pain, but I love Jesus alone. I wish Him to be the Master of my heart. Tell Him that I love Him and that I adore Him. Tell Him that I want to suffer, that I want to die of love and suffering, that the world doesn't interest me, just He alone. Yes, Mother. I'm alone. I unite myself to your solitude. Console me, nourish me, counsel me, be my companion and bless me.
>
> You are my Mother and I tell you that I'm in pain. Previously my pain had a truce, a ray of light in my dark heart; but this ray of light shines nor smiles for me. That smile of my mama made me live and I enjoyed it twice a week; but now I'll have it no longer. Tomorrow will be Wednesday and no one will call me to the parlour. Come with your Child, and my happiness will be complete.
>
> Help me to know my lessons, my reviews, my exams. Help me to win prizes to make you and my Jesus and my parents happy. Mary, my Mother, hear me. Your child.[181]

And she wrote to her school friend Elena:

Ask the Most Holy Virgin to be your guide to be your star, the lantern that shines for you amid the darkness of your life. May she show you the port where you must land to come to the heavenly Jerusalem.[182]

CHAPTER FOUR

What Does Suffering Matter If A Person Loves?

When Jesus revealed to Juanita her vocation to Carmel, He also revealed that her vocation would be one of suffering.

Suffering is one of the great mysteries of life, and one of the main reasons people say that they are unable to believe in God, especially not a loving God, for if He were a loving God, how could He allow such suffering and evil that there is in the world? Jesus Himself entered into this mystery and took the evil, sin and suffering on Himself in His death on the Cross. In our baptism, when we enter the waters to die and rise with Him and thus share in His risen life, we also pledge to follow Him: 'All I want is to know Christ and the power of his resurrection and to share his sufferings, by reproducing the pattern of his death'. (Philippians 3:10). The Catechism of the Catholic Church says:

> Now, however, 'we walk by faith, not by sight', we perceive God as 'in a mirror, dimly', and only 'in part'. Even though enlightened by him in whom we believe, faith is often lived in darkness and can be put to the test. The world we live in often seems very far from the one promised us by faith. Our experiences of evil and suffering, injustice and death, seem to contradict the Good News; they can shake our faith and become a temptation against it.
>
> It is then we must turn to the *witnesses of faith*:to Abraham, who 'in hope ... believed against hope', to the Virgin Mary, who in 'her pilgrimage of faith, walked into the 'night of faith', in sharing the darkness of her Son's suffering and death. (CCC 164, 165)

All Christians are called to walk in a 'night of faith', but it seems that certain souls are called to enter into, in a special and more intense manner, the mystery of suffering. We just have to think of our own young saints, St Thérèse of Lisieux and St Elizabeth of the Trinity, who experienced much suffering in their life and plumbed its depths, and to them is now joined Juanita. Our Lord willed for her a calling to suffering and in that calling gave her the desire for it. She set out some reasons as to why she was drawn to suffering:

> Suffering pleases me for two reasons: first, because Jesus always preferred suffering, from His birth till His death on the cross. It must be something very great because He, the all-powerful One, seeks suffering in all things. Second, it pleases me because in the crucible of suffering souls are formed. And because Jesus sends this gift that was so pleasing to Him to the souls He loves most.[183]

To Suffer with Joy

Juanita said that Jesus asked her to suffer and not complain, indeed, to suffer with joy. She understood that Jesus was calling her to suffering, and in her first letter to Mother Angelica said that 'I also know that if I go to Carmel it will be to suffer but suffering is nothing new or unknown to me'. As always, suffering is inextricably linked to love and prayer:

> In it I find my joy, for Jesus is on the cross and He is love. And what does suffering matter if a person loves? The life of a Carmelite is one of suffering loving and praying, and I find my whole idea in this, Rev. Mother. My Jesus has taught me these three things since I was a little girl. How grateful I should be to my Divine Master for the lessons He gives to someone as undeserving as me![184]

She would also have been drawn to what St Elizabeth of the Trinity said on the eve of her Profession: 'I understood that my Heaven was beginning on earth; Heaven in faith, with suffering and immolation for Him whom I love!'[185]

To suffer with joy goes right back to the pages of the New Testament. As St Peter said, 'Beloved, do not be surprised at the fiery ordeal that comes upon you, as though something strange were happening to you. But rejoice in so far as you share Christ's sufferings, that you may also rejoice and be glad when his glory is revealed'(1 Peter 4: 12-13); this is something the saints have echoed down the ages. From the very first, Christians knew that their sufferings were linked to the sufferings of Christ Himself.

St Thérèse cultivated the habit of smiling through whatever hurt her, so that no-one would know she was suffering. In the last months of Elizabeth's life a sister asked her if she was suffering a lot. Elizabeth's face grimaced to show the agony she was in, before she resumed her usual tranquil smile. Juanita also was - usually – able to retain her serenity to conceal her suffering.

St Paul has the mysterious sense that the afflictions of Christ, which have infinite value and are complete in themselves, are, in His Mystical Body of believers, insufficient until they are completed by those of believers, so closely are the two entwined: 'Now I rejoice in my sufferings for your sake, and in my flesh I complete what is lacking in Christ's afflictions for the sake of his body, that is, the church.' (Colossians 1:24)

Juanita learnt how to suffer joyfully, bit by bit, as she recounts soon after she went to the boarding school: 'Today, ever since I got up, I feel very sad, it seems suddenly my heart is breaking. Jesus told me that He wants me to suffer with joy. This costs me so, but it is sufficient that He asks this, so that I'll try to do it.'[186] Further on she notes, 'Today I promised my Jesus to fulfil His Divine Will by accepting with joy whatever He commands'.[187]

She was reading the works of St Elizabeth of the Trinity and meditating on the name Elizabeth had given herself 'The Praise of

Glory', (cf. Ephesians 1:12). She saw that to be a praise of glory was a work begun here on earth in the heaven of her soul and would be hers in eternity and this included times of suffering. 'She enchants me', wrote Juanita. 'Her soul is like mine. Though she was a saint, I'll imitate her and become a saint ... 'since Christ suffered His whole life long and was the praise of the glory of His Father, I'll suffer with joy for my sins and for sinners'.[188]

Juanita understood that her suffering with joy had a salvific dimension for others, not only for herself. She also began to realise that in embracing suffering, rather than fighting against it, it was becoming the very air she breathed: 'May my Jesus always lead me by the way of the Cross. And then my soul will take flight, where it can encounter the air that gives life and where there is repose'.[189]

In various places Juanita spoke of Jesus as her Captain, and she wanted to live up to that martial ideal:

> I'll joyfully fulfil the will of God in sadness and in joy, without ever betraying on my face what's going on in my heart. I'll never cry, ever keeping in mind the words of Saint Teresa: It's imperative to have the heart of a man and not that of a woman.[190]

Suffering in the Ordinary

At first glance it seems that Juanita's sufferings were not out of the ordinary: the death of her grandfather, adjusting to life in a boarding school, a serious illness, a change in the family's financial circumstances. They were events that could happen in any life. Was Juanita exaggerating her sufferings, giving them undue importance? To outsiders, she would seem highly favoured – she knew wealth, and they were not poverty-stricken, she was very attractive, popular, excelled at sports, highly intelligent and routinely coming top of her class.

Perhaps this highlights the fact that everyone has sufferings of one sort or another in their life, and the important thing is how to react to life's disappointments and difficulties. The lesson Jesus was teaching Juanita was to seek Him in all the circumstances of her life, and give to Him whatever He sends or permits, for the salvation of souls:

> I need your prayers more than ever, Rev, Mother, because I'm going through a time of trials. Our Lord wants me to seek Him alone, without looking for consolation of any kind in prayer. I'm giving Him thanks, for in this way I'm giving myself to Him without any mixture of selfishness, not because of His consolations, but because I love Him. Still, there are times of discouragement, and it seems to me that Our Lord only sends this to me because of my ingratitude. But I do want to fulfil God's will, and if He wants and is pleased, I intend to spend my whole life in this state of dryness, for the sake of sinners and priests.[191]

St Teresa of Avila adds a different perspective of the sufferings of Juanita, who was a contemplative and a mystic; she was receiving from the Lord the wine of His favours so that she could tread a 'rough and uneven path':

> Well, to think that He admits into His intimate friendship people who live in comfort and without trials is foolish. I am very certain that God gives contemplatives much greater trials. Thus, since He leads them along a rough and uneven path and at times they think they are lost and must return to begin again, His Majesty needs to give them sustenance, and not water but wine so that in their inebriation they will not understand what they are suffering and will be able to endure it. So, I see few true contemplatives who are not courageous and determined to suffer, for the first thing the Lord does, if they are weak, is to give them courage and make them unafraid of trials.[192]

Perhaps it is in this light that we can put Juanita's account of her time at school. Her diary is an unadorned descriptions of her physical, mental and spiritual sufferings, as well as the immense graces with which Our Lord was urging her along the way. It contrasts with the joyful letters she wrote to her friends, full of the love of God which she longed to share with them. Only to a few of her most intimate friends would she mention that she was having health problem or dryness in prayer, those who, like her, were intending to enter the religious life and understood the commitment and the love this called for.

It is as if in her diary we are in the 'engine-room' of her soul, where she describes her struggles, while her letters to friends show the serenity and joy she exuded to others. In her letters to priests she is open about her problems and the state of her soul, and these letters give a profound insight into her spiritual journey.

In the trials of her school life Our Lord was preparing her for the final stages of her spiritual journey in Carmel, where she lived to the full her life of prayer for souls, for sinners, for priests, and finding there the God of Infinite Joy who can be found only by those who embrace His Cross.

Trying to be Good

Trying to be good means that sometimes it backfires, something that Juanita experienced. On the one hand she says she is united to the Lord, and at the same time she wants to behave badly. But she is given the assurance that she was not culpable. Temptations, tests, are not sinful in themselves, and Our Lord knows our physical frailty:

> I've been very united to Our Lord. Still, I don't feel fervour. I've been very strange. I had a strong desire to behave badly, to become angry, finally, to the point of crying. I believe all that comes from

the way I feel physically. This morning I almost didn't make a meditation. And my thanksgiving after Communion was less than fervent, because I was exhausted. But Jesus told me that I shouldn't be upset, that I'm not culpable for this.[193]

Juanita's hunger to suffer stemmed for her intense love for Jesus, and anything could be used, even the smallest thing, to be offered up and given to Him, although sometimes it is the smallest things that are the most difficult to do. She had a sweet tooth and mentions that she was able to give up sweets for the whole of Holy Week, and then there was her weakness for caramels. She was trying to mortify herself, but:

> I've had such an unusual craving to eat caramels. Today I had such hunger that I ate all those I could and the ones that tasted best. It pains me to see that this is the way I am. truly I don't know what to do. I'll consult with Mother Izquierdo about this. Today I was very dissipated. What should I do with such misery.[194]

> Yesterday and today I have not eaten caramels, since I have offered them to Jesus, which pleases Him more than me'.[195]

Sweets were still causing her problems. She was tired and angry and needed a good sugar boost!

> Thursday October 18. Today I had to do a great deal to conquer myself. I was very angry, and sorry that I disobeyed and did my own will. I was weary and thought that I didn't have a vocation, that it was an illusion, just an idea I would afterward despair of; finally, so many things. But I prayed fervently to the Most Holy Virgin and in the depths of my soul I heard the voice of my Jesus: 'Learn of Me because I am meek and humble of heart.' And in this way my anger came to an end. Today one of the Sisters gave out

a box of candy and, since she gave me a small piece, it made me furious and I threw it away; and then I wouldn't accept the other piece she gave me. Dear Jesus, what do You say about this soldier who is so cowardly and so imperfect?[196]

Redemptive Suffering

Shortly before she left school, Juanita went to see the Mother Vicar, who gave her the advice that she shouldn't allow herself to be carried away by impressions and feelings, 'but always preserve a serene countenance, despite contradictions and sorrows'. This was something that Juanita had practiced for many years, gradually acquiring the serenity in her bearing that was so characteristic of her, not revealing the difficulties and pains she was going through inside. Even at school Juanita was being led through the desert of both physical and spiritual suffering:

> I can't do any more. Unless Jesus sustains me, I don't know what I'll do, because I'll be spending the whole day lying down and doing nothing but live in a state of confusion. I have a constant headache that makes me see everything in different colours. My God, Thy Will not mine be done. I offer You my sufferings for my sins, for sinners and for the sanctification of priests.
>
> Death, what is more desirable? To die and to live in God for an eternity and have fruition in God, can there be any greater happiness? My dear Jesus, every time I feel bad, I feel homesick for You and for that Heaven where I'll nevermore offend You; where I'll be inebriated with Your love, Jesus, where I'll be one with You, since I must have my being and movement in You.[197]

> Our Lord seems to want to test me during this course year, because I've been suffering quite a lot, and there's no one to go

to for advice. I have many doubts about my Carmelite vocation. Doubts, too, about faith, so that sometimes I ask myself if God exists, Rev. Father, as I felt so abandoned by Him. I looked at my crucifix and it all seemed like a trick of the mind. I cried and begged the Virgin's help, but she didn't help me, either. At last Our Lord took pity on me and allowed me to hear His voice in my heart. Then it was all over and I was filled with peace.[198]

Victim of love

On Trinity Sunday, 9 June 1895, during Mass, St Thérèse of Lisieux felt inspired to offer herself to Merciful Love. In the Act of Oblation that she wrote shortly afterwards, she offered herself to the Trinity as a victim of holocaust to Merciful Love. Juanita, too, was chosen to be a victim:

[Jesus] manifested His love to me, in such a way that I began to cry. He showed me His greatness and my nothingness, and told me He had chosen me as a victim. I must climb Calvary with Him, together we should undertake the conquest of souls: He the Captain, and I the soldier. Our motto, the cross. Our cry love. he told me that I should suffer with joy and with love, and every day I should remove a thorn from His Heart.[199]

Shortly before she entered Carmel, St Elizabeth of the Trinity said to a friend that she longed for suffering. 'Don't delude yourself, Elizabeth', the friend said'. 'God takes people like yourself at their word and accepts their self-giving'. 'I'm ready to take the plunge', replied Elizabeth. 'I hope I do suffer; that's what I'm entering Carmel for'.[200]

The Christian understanding of 'victim' has none of the passive connotations that it can have in the secular world. For Thérèse,

Elizabeth and Juanita it was an active and total self-giving to Jesus, in union with Him as the Lamb of God, offering Himself as the Victim to take away the sins of the world.

In the synoptic Gospels, we see Jesus being handed over to the Jewish and Roman authorities, but St John's Gospel shows Jesus at all times in control of what happens. Even at the very last, He takes a sip of the sour wine being handed to Him, because even such a small thing was prophesied and He had to fulfil all the prophesies about Himself. Only then could He hand Himself over to His Father and breathe His last. He was a willing victim: 'looking to Jesus the pioneer and perfector of our faith, who for the joy that was set before him endured the cross, despising the shame'. (Hebrews 12:2)

Our three young Carmelites freely gave themselves to divine Love for the salvation of souls. Even at school Juanita was being united ever more closely to Our Lord in His suffering. In a diary entry for June she records how close they were and how Jesus was revealing the cause of His suffering at that time:

> Last night He told me He was suffering greatly. He reclined on my heart and there He cried and I together with Him. A new persecution was beginning against Him, He told me, and said He loved us so much He was unable to live without us.[201]

This was a prophesy of the rise of Communism and Nazism during which millions of people would be killed and in which the Church would be mercilessly persecuted. In the death of countless millions it is Jesus Himself who was being persecuted and killed – and that persecution is still ongoing in many countries in the world. Jesus' love for all His children is unmeasured; His Sacred Humanity is in heaven and He can never forsake those to whom He is eternally united.

But it throws up an interesting question: how can it be that Jesus, who is now reigning in glory in the heaven where 'every tear will be wiped away' from the faces of those who have suffered, still be suffering? Likewise with the appearances of Our Lady, often seen in tears for her children? No sin, no pain, no suffering, can enter the all-embracing love of heaven which is theirs and yet they are portrayed as still suffering.

Every event in the life of Jesus, from His conception to His death and Resurrection, occurred at a specific time and in a specific place, because His was a fully human life. But because He is also fully Divine, every event in His human life, because He is God, has a divine and infinite dimension, outside of time and space. Therefore, when Jesus portrays Himself as suffering, that is His earthly suffering made present to us. When Mary is seen weeping, it is those tears she shed while on earth. In the Communion of Saints, all that a believer suffers on this earth likewise has an infinite value, outside of time and space, because united to the sufferings of Christ, which gives them that value.

The redemptive effects of Jesus' Passion stretched back into the past to bring the souls of the righteous into the heaven opened up by Christ's death and Resurrection. They apply today and into the future and He invites all his followers to share in His sufferings by uniting their suffering with His, as members of His Mystical Body.

CHAPTER SIX

This Darkness Is Followed By A Bit Of Light

Experience of union with God

Eleven days after she had entered the Los Andes Carmel, Teresa had an experience of mystical union with Our Lord. In describing her prayer we need to see her experiences in the light of what St Teresa of Avila describes in mansion 7 of The Interior Castle, because they will throw light on what Juanita now experiences in her prayer. She was made aware that her union with God was salvific: it would, like a magnet, draw other souls after her into union with Our Lord:

> May 17, 1919. I am greatly aware of divine love. In prayer I felt that the Sacred Heart was united to mine. And His love was so great that I felt my whole body embraced in that love and yet with no experience of my own body. All this touched me so that I had to sit down and a sensation so disagreeable was produced in me that I began to quiver. The love of God was manifested to me in such a way that I was unaware of what was happening. I spent almost an hour and three quarters in this way. Our Lord told me that I should abandon myself totally to Him and that I would attract many souls to abandon themselves completely. I offered myself as a victim so that He would manifest His infinite love to souls, he told me that I should do all this by uniting myself to Him.[202]

Writing to Fr Blanch 10 November, Juanita describes her prayer as going from love to darkness. From the very beginning this alternation is there, and we have to see what God was doing in her:

> The state of my soul is such that I can't define it; one day darkness, distractions, with my will longing to love, causing me great pain at my inability to love Our Lord, my inability to see Him. Here I can't keep back my tears, because I cry out to my Jesus with such anguish. Another day, I'm able to be recollected in faith, but don't feel anything. All I can do is meditate. This darkness is followed by a bit of light which increases my torment. I also feel my sinfulness and my inconstancy so much that I begin to hate myself, and it seems to me that no one loves me, which causes me to suffer, since I find neither consolation or peace in God or in creatures. I see the immense love of my God, and feel myself incapable of loving Him according to the longings within me. I want to suffer, yet resign myself to the divine will.[203]

The Dark Night

The Dark Night for those who have achieved the highest union with God takes on a different dimension. It is no longer primarily for the purification of the mind, soul and spirit, although always some faults remain, but there is a salvific aspect to it to an even greater degree than before, when sufferings are offered up to God for souls. As an example, let us look at the trial of faith of St Thérèse of Lisieux:[204]

> During those very joyful days of the Easter season, Jesus made me feel that there were really souls who have no faith, and who, through the abuse of grace, lost this precious treasure, the source of the only real and pure joys. He permitted my soul to be invaded by the thickest darkness, and that the thought of heaven, up until then so sweet to me, be no longer anything but the cause of a struggle

and torment. This trial was to last not a few days or a few weeks, it was not to be extinguished until the hour set by God Himself and this hour has not yet come …

Your child, however, O Lord, has understood Your divine light, and she begs pardon for her brothers. She is resigned to eat the bread of sorrow as long as You desire it; she does not wish to rise up from this table filled with bitterness at which poor sinners are eating until the day set by You …

Never have I felt before this, dear Mother, how sweet and merciful the Lord really is, for He did not send me this trial until the moment I was capable of bearing it. A little earlier I believe it would have plunged me into a state of discouragement.

A few things can be noted here. Thérèse was given this trial of faith only when she was able to bear it – until she was firmly rooted in the love of God: she had received the dart of divine love in the choir- the mystical marriage – a short while before. She understood that this trial was being given to her so that she could unite herself with unbelievers and have a mystical share, a salvific union, in the bitterness of their unbelief.

Juanita's Fourfold Trial

We now consider the experiences Juanita had in the light of Thérèse's experience. She first receives a vision of Our Lord's agony which is more graphic than any she had received before. This was surely the great suffering of which Our Lord had spoken and was now being enacted within her soul:

26 May. For 3 days I've been taken into Our Lord's agony. He is represented to me at each instant as dying, with His face on the

ground. His hair is red with blood. His eyes are vivid. Without a countenance. He is pallid and emaciated. His tunic covers only half of His body. His back is covered with a multitude of lance wounds, which I understood are sins. In His shoulder blades He has two wounds that allow us to see His white bones, and nailed to the holes of these wounds are lances that hurt Him horribly. On both sides the blood flows down in torrents, inundating the ground. The Most Holy Virgin was standing by His side, weeping and asking the Father for mercy. I see this image with such vividness that it produces in me a kind of agony. I can't cry, but perspiration pours over me and my hands grow cold and my heart pains me so that I feel shortness of breath.[205]

After describing the above experience she then gave a description of a series of tests which humbled her deeply. These occurred during the Cenacle retreat, between another experience of union with the Trinity:

Today, before the feast of Pentecost, I felt my whole being carried off in God with great violence, without being able to conceal it. Three times I returned to myself and was then again transported. I suffer greatly, since I don't know if these are illusions, and I don't have anyone to consult about this matter. Finally, I surrender myself to God's will. He's my Father, my Spouse, my Sanctifier. He loves me and desires my well-being.[206]

Between those two graces Our Lord united her to Himself in His Passion in four stages. In the first, she had had to accompany Our Lord in His agony of sins piercing His Body. Then, in the second trial:

horrible doubts against faith came to me so that I was tempted not to go to Communion and afterward, when I had the Sacred Form on my tongue, I wanted to spit it up, because I thought Our Lord was not there nor had He ever existed there. I didn't know what was happening to me and I asked our Mother Superior about this. She assured me that I hadn't given consent. With that I remained more at peace and she told me that I should pay no attention to that thought. Thus the temptation disappeared. But our Mother Superior told me that I should be more of a woman. Our Lord reproached me for discharging my cross onto our Mother Superior, and He asked me to suffer without saying anything.[207]

It is possible that here Our Lord was allowing Juanita to experience two of the greatest sorrows that caused Him so much agony in the garden: 'doubts against faith'. Was it this that caused Our Lord to sweat drops like blood at the thought that the agony, pain, mockery and death he was shortly to undergo would be as nought for so many, who would disbelieve, reject and mock that total gift of Himself that he was offering?

Then, shortly before, He had given Himself under the form of bread and wine, the gift of His very self in the Sacrament of the Eucharist, at the Last Supper. It was only God who could conceive and bring about such a thing. But Jesus knew that so many, like those in John 6:66, even his close followers, would be so disgusted at the thought of eating His Body and drinking His blood, an assertion He refused to soften, that they would turn away and leave Him. In this trial Juanita, who had such a profound conviction and depth of understanding of the Eucharist, was experiencing in herself this rejection of belief in the reality of the presence of Christ in the consecrated Host.

Mother Angelica assured Juanita that she had not given consent to this temptation, but that she told her to be 'more of a woman' seems to imply that at this point she didn't understand exactly what Juanita was experiencing. In all the letters Juanita had written to her before her entry into Carmel, she never mentioned the extraordinary favours she had been receiving, so it would have taken the Prioress some while to understand what was happening. In the community, it was only herself, the Sister Preceptor and a fellow novice who had seen her in ecstasy, who would know of the exceptional favours and trials Juanita was receiving.

Also, Our Lord was telling Juanita not to seek the consolation of telling the Prioress of her crosses – and Juanita herself had already understood that she should bear her crosses in silence. Sometimes, though, the weight of them became too much for her to bear and she had to seek human consolation.

Before she entered Carmel, Fr Blanch gave her instructions that she should never give an account of the state of her soul to the Mistress of novices and her Superior, nor of the special inspirations given by Our Lord, 'because afterward I would remain uneasy'. Also, that if she had temptations or scruples, she should always speak of them to her confessor or another priest, because God gives them light, because he considered that only a priest had the training to guide her. This did become a problem for Juanita later on and how much she should reveal to her Prioress.

The third trial revealed to her the weight of her sins:

> My third trial was most horrible. I felt the whole weight of my sins, as well as God's numerous favours and love. I still didn't know what was happening in seeing that I didn't correspond to Our Lord. My pain increased more in the refectory when I hear what the primitive monks did. I began to cry in my cell, being prostrate, with my head on the ground. That's the way I was when Our Mother came looking for me to go into the garden and she kept me conversing all during the recreation period. I was unable to do more; but I didn't tell her nor did I give her a reason to suspect. Quite the contrary. That night she asked me if I was peaceful and I told her yes, since I was so united with God's will, and I was overwhelmed by God's graces. She told me to go to bed, and that was worse, since I saw that Our Lord didn't even want me to praise Him. Afterward I remained with such pain that it was horrible. On the following day Our Lord presented Himself to me when He was not in His agony, but with His face so sad. I asked Him what was wrong, but He didn't answer me, making me understand that He

was angry with me. But afterward, as I persisted in asking Him, He told me that He didn't want to speak to me, and that I was a sinner. He told me all the sins of my life in a moment and He continued to be very sad. I remained with great pain and confused because of my sins. But I was unable to believe that He was angry, since He had told me that He had pardoned me. And, furthermore, He's all goodness and mercy.[208]

It is true that the closer a soul gets to the light of God, the darker do her sins and faults appear. Juanita often called herself a criminal nothingness, but not here. She said that during this trial she is confused because she knows God has forgiven her, so in this instance there is no ordinary sense in which she felt the weight of her sinfulness. In this trial she was not overwhelmed as God revealed her sins. She was 'so united with God's will, and 'I was overwhelmed by God's graces'. Perhaps we should see it in the light of St Thérèse's experience of eating the bread of unbelievers. Here, Juanita is sharing mystically the lot of the sinner, who feels as if God is angry with him and cut off from the love of God. But there is no sense of despair here because Juanita knows God loves her, and she is giving the message that every sinner should know likewise and trust in that love.

The fourth trial led her deeper into darkness:

The fourth trial was terrifying. It took place after prayer when I saw myself inflamed and transported to God, without being able to move. The thought came to me that all this was the deceit of the devil, and the proof was that I had not obeyed the bell. The darknesses were most horrible, since I believed that I was without God's protection. Furthermore, I felt the greatest pain in seeing that all were noticing something strange in me. This filled me with pain, since I desire to remain unnoticed.[209]

This was such a painful trial for Juanita, afraid that all she was experiencing was of the devil, a fear that she had had before but never in such darkness. Even a small fault can make us feel that God doesn't love us, but it is also a reminder that He asks for our faithfulness. Living in a secular world with faith and belief consigned mainly to the peripheries, it can be easy to think that our faith is not real, that secular ways of thinking are the reality. In her humility Juanita didn't want others to know of the favours she was receiving, to make her 'stand out' in the community.

In these series of experiences, Jesus was drawing Juanita into an ever-closer union with the thirst for souls He had, and in return she offered up to Him all that she was.:

> How happy I feel when I can tell Him: 'Everything I am belongs to You, my Jesus. My heart must only love You and love souls, since these are sprinkled with Your blood. When I sacrifice myself for them, I but sacrifice myself in order to gather up Your adorable blood that it may not be lost. And so, I do save souls, but without losing sight of You, my divine Star. My intelligence, my thinking, my memory belong to You. I have no need to know created things nor to study human wisdom. You are my Wisdom, my book of eternal Truth. My body, too, I have come to offer up, because I love You, and because from the cross You teach me to crucify it.[210]

Juanita's Visions

What was the nature of Juanita's visions? She said that she always saw Jesus in His sufferings; the only exception was the vision she saw of Him in the chapel during her first visit to the Carmel. She uses various expressions to describe her experiences: 'He is represented to me'; 'Our Lord presented Himself to me'. It seems from this that Juanita's visions are what St Teresa of Avila calls 'intellectual visions', that is, the vision is not as if it was external to the one receiving it, but internally. This is different from when we imagine a scene from the Gospel, for example, when, as St Ignatius describes, we enter as fully as we can into the scene, imagining the scents, the smells, the different people, how we would react, etc. In St Teresa's words:

> Although I say 'image' let it be understood that, in the opinion of the one who sees it, it is not a painting but truly alive, and sometimes the Lord is speaking to the soul and even revealing great secrets. But you must understand that even though the soul is detained for some while, it can no more fix its gaze on the vision than it can on the sun.[211]

Juanita described with great precision some experiences she had to Fr Falgueras in the important Letter 87. The first vision was an intellectual one and became deeply engraved in her soul:

> Once, at night, just before I went to sleep, after I made my examination of conscience, Our Lord revealed Himself to me with such vividness that it seemed I could see Him. He was crowned with thorns and His face was so sorrowful that I could not contain myself and began to cry so much that the Lord then had to console me in the intimate depths of my soul. This lasted for two minutes, more or less, and His face remained engraved for a long time in my memory.

Juanita thought she had produced a vision of Our Lady through her imagination, but the circumstances surrounding it seem that it was a genuine vision: everything around her vanished, it lasted a very short time but was recalled with great precision; she did not see Our Lady's face, but it was an answer to her prayer: that her prayer was truly accepted in heaven. This is a great confirmation from heaven that God and the saints really do hear our prayer:

> And another time when I was praying some 'Ave Marias' to make a crown for the Most Holy Virgin, everything disappeared from my sight and I saw over my Mother's head a crown filled with precious stones which gave off rays of light, but I didn't see her face. I think this was produced by my imagination, since it lasted but a second, and besides I'd been wanting to know if the Most Holy Virgin really accepted my prayers.

The third vision introduced her into the profound reality of the Blessed Sacrament and bound her own life closely to the Eucharistic Mystery:

> Twice Our Lord revealed Himself and His love to me in the Most Blessed Sacrament, but in an almost sensible way. Once He made me understand His grandeur and told me then how He humbled Himself under the form of bread. This happened while I was at school … Last year Our Lord represented Himself to me with His face filled with sorrow and a prayerful attitude; and His eyes were raised to heaven. His hand was over His Heart. He told me He was praying incessantly to His Father for sinners, and that He offered Himself for them there on the altar. He told me to do the same, and He assured me that in the future I would live more united with Him. He said that He had chosen me with a special preference over other souls, since He wanted me to live by suffering and consoling Him throughout my life.[212]

Are Visions Real?

Such experiences can be and often are, dismissed as the products of an overwrought imagination, and even as mental illness. They can be. But in the case of the visions of saints we need to take them seriously. The Church says that we do not have to believe them, even when they are officially approved by the Church, such as the visions of Our Lord to St Margaret Mary or the appearances of Our Lady to St Bernadette and the Fatima children. This is even more true when they are private visions, such as those given to Juanita. Nevertheless, we are encouraged to think about them and think about the truths of the Faith that they reveal to us in greater depth than we might think of for ourselves.

How can someone know whether a vision is real or not? Firstly, seek the advice of an experienced priest or spiritual director, because he will be trained to know whether what is being received is true or not. Then, a genuine vision will never contradict a truth of the Faith. In *The Interior Castle V1:9*, St Teresa gives valuable advice. A true vision, she says, even if to begin with, 'it arouses great fear and tumult', the result is a 'happy peace … all remains calm, and this soul is left so well instructed about so many great truths that it has no need of any other master.' Through the many favours Juanita received she had a deep understanding of her faith and the ability to share it with others with great beauty, clarity and conviction. Theology has been described as 'faith seeking understanding', and in the solid grounding she received at school, coupled with her ardent love of God, she never ceased seeking to understand more deeply the person of Jesus Christ and her faith in Him.

St Teresa continues: 'without any effort on the soul's part, true Wisdom has taken away the mind's dullness and leaves a certitude'. A true vision has the solidity of heaven about spiritual things, beyond what ordinary intelligence can provide, but always faith and reason are inseparable. The reason can be transcended but never negated. Sometimes, St Teresa says, the devil can cause the soul to waver and doubt, but he cannot destroy the soul's certitude and the acknowledgement that such favours bring blessings and spiritual growth.

CHAPTER SEVEN
The Perfection Of Love

Before she entered Carmel, Juanita described a prayer she made 'because Our Lord told me this' on the Blessed Trinity, the supreme Mystery to which Our Lord would progressively introduce her:

> My meditation was, because Our Lord told me this, about the Three Divine Persons; how the Father, by knowing Himself, engendered the Word and, by loving Himself, the Holy Spirit, and the operations that each Person exercises in souls.[213]

Juanita had already reached a high degree of holiness before she entered Carmel. She was being introduced to the mystical betrothal with Jesus. St Teresa of Avila describes it:

> The betrothal itself takes place when His Majesty gives the raptures that draws it out of its senses. For if it were to see itself so near this great majesty while in its senses, it would perhaps die. Though the soul in ecstasy is without consciousness in its outward life, it was never before so awake to the things of God nor did it ever before have so deep an enlightenment and knowledge of God.[214]

In Carmel Our Lord was drawing her to the heights of mystical union with Himself in the Mystical Marriage.

In June the community went into a retreat between the Ascension and

Pentecost, and it seems that it was during this time that she experienced what could be the Mystical Marriage:

> God is communicating Himself to my soul in so ineffable a way during these days in the Cenacle [the Upper Room of the Last Supper]. The love I feel is not sensible, but much more interior. In prayer there are things happening that never happened before: I remain completely steeped in God. I can't make reflective prayer. It's as though I'm sleeping in God. In this way I experience His greatness and so great is the joy I'm experiencing in my soul, as something coming from God. It seems to me that I find I'm completely immersed in the divinity.
>
> Three or four days ago while I was at prayer, I felt God was abasing Himself to me, but with such a great impetus of love that I believe that if it had lasted just a little more I'd have been unable to endure it, because in that moment my soul was about to leave my body. My heart was beating with such violence that it was awful. I felt that my whole being was as though suspended and that it was united to God. They rang the bell and I didn't hear it. I saw the other novices leave and I tried to follow them but was unable to move. It was as though I were nailed to the ground. Almost on the point of tears I begged Our Lord to allow me to leave since all were going to notice this. Then I was able to get up, but my soul was if in another place.[215]

This resembles what St Teresa of Avila describes as the Spiritual Marriage:

> In the spiritual marriage, there is still much less remembrance of the body because this secret union takes place in the very interior centre of the soul, which must be where God Himself is, and in my opinion there is no need of any door for Him to enter. I say there is no need of any door because everything that has been said up

until now seems to take place by means of the sense and faculties, and this appearance of the humanity of the Lord must also. But that which comes to pass in the union the spiritual marriage is very different. The Lord appears in this centre of the soul, not in an imaginative vision but in an intellectual one, although more delicate than those mentioned, as He appeared to the apostles without entering through the door when He said to them *pax vobis*. What God communicates here to the soul in an instant is a secret so great and a favour so sublime – and the delight the soul experiences so extreme – that I don't know what to compare it to. I can say only that the Lord wishes to reveal for that moment, in a more sublime manner than through any spiritual vision or taste, the glory of heaven.[216]

Juanita's union with God was becoming more and more profound. Previously she had written to Fr Cea that she could not penetrate the immense furnace of the Holy Trinity; now, she can plunge into that furnace, aflame with Its light and love:

> The other day while I was praying, God told me to adore Him constantly in my soul, by offering Him the praise of all creatures and joining myself to the praise being offered to Him in heaven by the angels and saints. I've carried everything He told me to do and live much more united with Him in this way. I contemplate the Most Blessed Trinity in my soul, like an immense furnace of fire and light, which, because of its great intensity, I cannot penetrate or look upon. I can see the Blessed Virgin there and the angels and saints. I can also see myself there, a miserable creature, lost and annihilated before His Divine Majesty, and I unite myself with the praises that everyone in heaven is offering Him. He asked me to make this adoration of mine a constant thing, to make this praise uninterruptedly. I must do it in such a way that whether I speak or perform any actions whatsoever, I should do it for the sake of obtaining His greater glory.[217]

She could write to her friend Carmen Ortúzar, that she is now immersed in the bosom of the Most Holy Trinity; the Sacred Heart of Jesus is the entry, the door, through which she enters into the very being of God, which is Love:

> So I invite you, Carmen, to enter into His Divine Heart, where I live submerged, breathing only on the divine, and consuming my many miseries in the fire of His love. That's where I live, contemplating the grandeur of His Divinity. First, I look at God – that incomparable Trinity – plunging myself into the bosom of my Father, of my Spouse, of my Sanctifier, and then I look at the eternal Word made flesh, at my Divine Jesus. That's when I sing my praise of glory and of love.[218]

As St Teresa of Avila said, the spiritual marriage consists in this high union of the soul with the Blessed Trinity:

> Our good God now desires to remove the scales from the soul's eyes and let it see and understand, although in a strange way, something of the favour He grants it. When the soul is brought into that dwelling place, the Most Blessed Trinity, all three Persons, through an intellectual vision, is revealed to it through a certain representation of the truth.[219]

St John tells us: 'even in this world we are like him' (1 John 4:17). In these few words he tells us what transforming union is, transformation into Jesus Christ by sharing His Spirit and being perfected in that love which drives out fear.

In her life Juanita shows us how she became transfigured, transformed into the Lord she loved, driven by His own love within her. In times of dryness and darkness love impelled her to seek Him Whom she loved;

in times of light and joy Love impelled her to try to give love for Love, by that Love which lived in her. What St John writes of in his letter applies to every baptized Christian; we are all called to experience that transforming love:

> Six days ago [6 August, feast of the Transfiguration] while I was making my thanksgiving after Communion, I felt so great a love for Our Lord that it seemed to me my heart could not resist it. Yet at the same time – believe me, Father, I don't know how to express what happened to me – I felt kind of stunned, throughout those days I've been as though I were outside myself. I spent all those days as though I were not in myself. I would do things, but without realizing it. Later, in prayer, God would present Himself to me, but immediately my soul seemed to go out of itself. This happened with such violence that I nearly fell to the ground. I don't lose the use of my senses, for I hear what's happening around me, but I'm never distracted from God.[220]

As she described to Fr Crea in the letter quoted above, her spiritual journey alternated between light and darkness, but often the pain she felt was that she was unable to love as Him as deserved to be loved and how she wished to love Him. In a letter to her friend Ines Pereira, Juanita gives some idea of how completely she is united now in God, in the Spiritual Marriage:

> How clearly I sense that He's the only Good who can satisfy us, the only ideal who can make us fall completely in love. In Him I find everything. I rejoice to the infinite depths of my being to see Him so beautiful, to experience that I'm always united with Him, for God is immense and present everywhere. Nothing can separate me from Him. His divine essence is my life. At every moment God sustain and nourishes me. Everything I see speaks to me of His infinite power and love. By uniting myself with His Divine Being I sanctify myself, become perfect, and become divinized. Finally, I

tell you He's immutable, that He doesn't change and that His love for me is infinite – an eternal, incomprehensible love that led Him to become man, that made Him be transformed into bread in order to be with me, to suffer and console me.[221]

Mother Angelica had a firm belief in the holiness of her beloved charge. After Juanita's death she wrote the circular letter in which she described her beloved daughter:

> Our little sister, who from her earliest years had exercised herself in acquiring and practicing virtue impelled by her love of Jesus, appeared to have mastered them all. Thus, we could see, it might be said, a consummate prudence and discretion united with an angelic simplicity in this child. In her conversations she expressed herself with naturalness, without reticence, or measuring words. She was affable and joyful. She always strove to hide her intelligence and evident talent, the solid instruction she had received, and the enlightenment on the highest matters which God's grace had given her. She made a concentrated effort in this matter. Using her favourite expression, she 'tried to efface herself' and wanted to be overshadowed. She never gave her opinion on anything. She was always ready to concede. She did not display knowledge of anything in matters of prayer, virtue, etc., although she had received instruction in them from God Himself.[222]

Juanita received exceptional graces in her ascent to union with God, and through those exceptional graces showed us by example that the ascent to transforming love is the norm for all Christians. But what Juanita describes of her union of love seems to be so far above what we ourselves normally experience may cause us to be discouraged. But we can bear in mind that in His parables Jesus often points to degrees of graces that are given to different people. Each one of us is unique, with different gifts of God: we might be given one talent, or two or five; we might bear fruit thirty-fold, sixty-fold or a hundred-fold. The important thing is that we use to the full the gifts and graces we have been given.

Even more important is the quality of our love. If we resolve to love Him to the full, then He will increase our capacity to receive even more of His love. We must not put limits on how much we can love God, because He puts no limits on His love for us. God, the Most Blessed Trinity, will continually stun us by the immensity of love that He has for us and that He wants to pour into us. That is Juanita's message to us:

> Let us love eternal Love, infinite and immutable Love.
> Let's love God madly for He loved us in His eternity.[223]

PART THREE

AFTERWARD

Live In Love, Live In Heaven, Live In God

Among the thousands of people gathered in St Peter's Square as the banner of the latest saint was unfurled, among the hundreds of people from Chile who had made the journey, was an elderly Sacred Heart sister, Anita Rucker, Juanita's cousin. Sitting there, she could only marvel that someone she had played with as a child, had studied with in school and enjoyed holidays with, was now proclaimed a saint. She felt that Juanita's influence helped her to fulfil her own vocation, a testimony to Juanita's influence after her death:

> Juanita became a religious before I did. The reason is because in our family there were only two girls, and so my father absolutely forbade either of us to enter religious life. Juanita died some time later and her death had a great impact on many people, including my own father. As a result, shortly after Sister Teresa's death, my father allowed me to become a religious of the Sacred Heart. In this way my cousin helped my vocation.[224]

Many decades later and now a Sister of the Sacred Heart, Anita described her thoughts as she attended the canonization of her cousin:

> When I saw that great banner hanging from the façade of Saint Peter's, with Teresa's beautiful picture on it, I could only ask

myself, is it true that I'm really seeing a cousin of mine and a companion at the Sacred Heart boarding school on Maestranza Street being raised to the altar? And then she slowly added; We didn't know the treasure we had so close to us, one we sometimes failed to understand. Detachment and devotion to God's will were her aim. All her joys and sorrows were transformed by this single ideal.

Perhaps in her pocket she had the treasured letter Juanita had written to her not long before she died, speaking of Anna's desire to enter the Sacred Heart Sisters. While she was waiting for that, Juanita wrote, 'still, I would like to suggest to you another vocation that I think you'll like, and it is that you be a religious of the Sacred Heart in your apostolic works of zeal and that you be a Carmelite, always living with God in the depths of your soul ... This isn't a new vocation. It's a special one for you. You must possess God that you may give Him to others.[225]

Pope St John Paul 11 said of her:

In her short life of little more than 19 years, in her 11 months as a Carmelite, God made shine forth in her in an admirable way the light of his Son Jesus Christ, so that she could be a beacon and guide to a world which seems to be blind to the splendour of the divine. In a secularized society which turns its back on God, this Chilean Carmelite whom to my great joy I present as a model of the perennial youth of the Gospel, gives the shining witness of a life which proclaims to the men and women of our day that it is in loving, adoring and serving God that the human person finds greatness and joy, freedom and fulfilment.[226]

The Journey to her Canonization

Juanita's funeral took place two days after her death. The Carmelite Vicar Provincial celebrated the Mass, accompanied by the Superior of the Heart of Mary and Carmelite fathers of Valparaiso and Santiago. The chaplain, parish priest and representatives of the Assumptionists, Passionists and Salesians accompanied her to the cemetery. There was a sense that there was something different and special about her death. People began to pass their rosaries and other devotionals through to the sisters so that they could be touched on Juanita's body. There was even an item in the local newspaper.

The news of her death spread rapidly throughout Santiago; in her old school bells were tolled and a solemn commemorative ceremony was held. Mother Maria Teresa Alaysa gave a moving address:

> We must give the Lord everything and increase our love for Him. And we must do it doubly because here on earth there is now emptiness. Gone is a little soul who glorified Him so. True, this is exactly what she is doing now in heaven, but Jesus is looking down from heaven on this earth sees a little less love.[227]

Her reputation for holiness spread rapidly, which was unusual, given the circumstances. She died in a poor, run-down Carmel which she chose deliberately because it was in a remote area. She was buried in the cloister, below the nun's choir, inaccessible to the public. The circular sent round after her death was sent only to other Carmels. A biography written about her was not a best-seller; nevertheless, her reputation spread; there were reports of prayer answered, even miracles.

It was among the young people that she found her most enthusiastic followers. Here was someone they could relate to, who loved sports, loved horse riding, who thrilled at the beauty of the Chilean landscape. Here was a young girl who laughed and giggled with friends at school, writing their letters to each other in code so the nuns couldn't read them. Here was a lovely young girl, popular, kind, studying at school, just one of them – but with that radiance, that reserve that told them that she had a special relationship with Our Lord that was out of the ordinary. Now, she could help them, she could show them how to become holy, to love the Lord, in their own lives.

In Chile, she was so popular that it was said that there was no house that didn't have a picture of her on the wall, and more than a million people visit her tomb annually, especially young people.

It was among those closest to her, that her influence first began to be felt. Because she put Jesus first in her life, even before her mother and father and family, despite the pain she caused to them as well as to herself, then, because of her family's own openness to God, their lives flourished in the love of God in a way they might not have done if Juanita had not given herself so totally to God. Her beloved father returned to the practice of his faith, dying a holy death three years later. Luis, too, found his faith again, and became an eminent lawyer. Miguel, although he never abandoned his bohemian lifestyle, likewise never forsook his faith and had published a volume of his poems. He married and had two children. Lucia and Chiro had another daughter, Laura, and they raised their children in a deeply Christian home. Ignatio worked in a bank and did voluntary work, he was married, with three children, living a fully Christian life. Doña Lucia, for all her heartbreaks and worries as her children grew up, could only rest in grateful thanks to God that, through the influence and the prayers of her beloved daughter, her husband and all her children lived Christian lives, each in their own ways.

However, the greatest transformation was in Rebecca. Rebecca described how it was as if a grey cloud of depression hung over her during Juanita's time in Carmel. At the moment of her death the cloud lifted, and with the lightness came into her Juanita's own vocation to Carmel. In the last letter she wrote to her sister Juanita seemed already to draw her in:

I want you to know how happy I am to belong to God alone, and

I'll tell you a secret: I see God working marvellously in your soul to draw you to himself, taking you away from the ones you love so much, separating you from everything so that you may find your only support in Him ... Live in love, live in heaven, live in God. This is the only happiness of your Carmelite sister's soul.[228]

Only a few months later Rebecca entered the Los Andes Carmel herself. Many of Juanita's friends also entered the religious life, Carmen Ortuzar, Marta Valdes and Amelia Martinez became Carmelites, Elena Gonzalez as well as Anna Rutter, became a Sacred Heart Sister.

Los Andes Carmel

After Teresa's death, the original Carmel where Teresa spent her life was damaged by an earthquake in 1924 and a larger Carmel was built. The Community moved in 1940 to a new monastery on Sarmiento Street and the remains of Sr Teresa were transferred to a new tomb in the Monastery choir.

Her popularity grew especially when, on 17 October 1947, the process of beatification began. In 18 March 1986 the Congregation of Cardinals and Bishops recognised that Sr Teresa of Jesus of Los Andes practiced the evangelical virtues to an heroic degree. As always in such proceedings, that she received extraordinary experiences such as locutions and visions had no part in this decision, only the fruit they produced of love, self-sacrifice and humility. Fr Valentino Macca was appointed Relator of her Cause and one of the aspects he had to examine was whether she was a true mystic:

> This we fully recognise her notable attainment of psychological and moral equilibrium. This accomplishment enabled her to become an authentic Discalced Carmelite. She was a woman of an intensely contemplative life who was centred in the full Teresian

spirit of courage. She was nourished by vital contact with Jesus Christ, love for her Carmelite vocation and by the apostolic understanding that she possessed.

All the documents affirm the mystical life of the Servant of God and deserve an essential value that goes beyond the phenomena that are very discreetly proposed in the Process.[229]

On 22 March Pope St John Paul 11 signed the decree recognizing the heroic nature of her virtues, officially declaring her 'Venerable'.

1st Miracle

For a person to be declared Blessed a miracle is required; a miracle, related by the mother, was approved 25 February 1987.

On December 4 1963, my son went (as a volunteer fireman) to a fire. During the course of fighting the fire his leg accidentally touched an electricity cable and he was electrocuted. He fell to the ground with a heart attack and was quickly rushed to the Central Headquarters. There he was diagnosed as having cerebral and pulmonary oedema. When they called me to Central Headquarters I was told he was very ill and the doctor told me that there was no hope. Then on the 8th December I went to Los Andes (where Teresa's tomb was then located) and I asked her to intercede for him so that he would live, even if he were only a vegetable. When I returned to Central Headquarters, the doors where usually no one is allowed entrance were open. The doctor called me and said there was no hope. I asked permission to see him and when I entered I found him on machines. He was unconscious. I approached and began speaking to him, and begged him to keep on fighting, then I kissed him on the forehead. All at once he moved very abruptly. I called the nurse and they made me leave.

During the night the captain of the firemen called me to notify me that they had disconnected the respirator. They went back connecting and disconnecting it, and the next day he was breathing on his own.

On December 19th he returned home totally cured. We then made a pilgrimage with the firemen. He led the way and we walked from Huechurabo to Los Andes. Now, he is feeling fine and every December 8th we gather to give thanks.[230]

The miracle was approved 25 February 1987, and 16th March Pope St John Paul 11 signed the decree for her solemn Beatification. He himself presided over the outdoor ceremony of Beatification in O'Higgins Park in Santiago, that was marred by young protesters and demonstrators who wanted, during the brutal Pinochet era, to draw attention to their political demands.

The Pope began his homily by quoting from St Paul: 'There are three things that last, faith, hope and love, and the greatest of these is love', emphasising that all her life Juanita was motivated and driven by love of her Lord, 'captivated by the heavenly Kingdom in the springtime of her life':

The secret of her life completely directed toward holiness is summarized in familiarity with Christ as a Friend who is constantly present, and with the Virgin Mary, a close and loving Mother.

Ever since she was a child, Teresa of Los Andes experienced the grace of communion with Christ, which developed within her with the charm of her youth. She was full of vitality and cheerfulness, never lacking a sense of healthy amusement and play, and contact with nature, just as a true daughter of her time. She was a happy and dynamic young girl, open to God. And God made Christian love blossom in her, an open love profoundly sensitive to the problems of her country and the aspirations of the Church.

The secret of her perfection could be none other than love; a great love for Christ, who fascinate her and moves her to consecrate herself to Him forever and to participate in the mystery of His Passion and Resurrection. At the same time she finds a filial love for the Virgin Mary, who draws her to imitate her virtues.

For her, God is infinite joy. This is the new hymn of Christian love that rises spontaneously from the soul of this young Chilean girl, in whose glorified face we can sense the grace of transformation in Christ. She possessed an understanding, serving, humble and patient love, a love which does not destroy human values, but rather elevates and transfigures them.[231]

Canonization

That same year, on 18th October 1987, the community moved to their new purpose-built monastery in Rinconada de Los Andes, ten miles away, where they are now. It is situated on land once owned by Juanita's grandfather, part of the hacienda of Chacabulco, where she had spent so many wonderful holidays.

On 11th December 1988, Juanita's remains were brought to their definitive resting place at Chacabuco on land Doñated by her relative, Luis Alberto Fernandes. On her tomb are inscribed the words Pope St John Paul 11 used in his homily to the pilgrims who came for the Canonization, 'Love is stronger than all things'.

The following day, 12th December, feast of Our Lady of Guadalupe, Patroness of Latin America, Cardinal Fresno, Archbishop of Santiago, consecrated the National shrine in honour of Our Lady of Mount Carmel, where the remains of Teresa of Los Andes are preserved.

The following year 13th July was officially assigned as her liturgical feast-day.

2nd Miracle

For Canonisation a second miracle is required. This occurred December 1968 during a school outing to celebrate the end of the school year. Some of the girls were enjoying themselves round the pool. Marcel Antunes Riveros, who was not an expert swimmer, turned over and ended up at the bottom of the pool without anyone realising she was in difficulties. When, five minutes later, her friends realised what had happened, she was brought up from the pool; she was not breathing, her heartbeat was light and almost imperceptible, and her eyes were glazed. Some mothers in the group immediately began praying to Juanita. According to the Medical Council, because she was asphyxiated, and water had entered her lungs, she should have suffered grave neurological and psychic damage due to the serious de-oxygenation of her blood.

Instead, after a 45-minute examination, Marcel was declared cured and perfectly healthy, both neurologically and psychologically.

This paved the way for Juanita's canonization, at which Marcel and her family were present.

On 11 July 1992 Pope St John Paul 11 signed the decree which approved the miracle, and on 21 March 1993, he celebrated the canonization of St Teresa of Jesus of Los Andes in St Peter's Basilica. It was the fourth Sunday of Lent, in which the account of the man born blind from the Gospel of John was read. The Pope used that incident to stress the importance of baptism as the gateway to the light of Christ and the community of the Church, referring it to the life of Teresita, as she is affectionately called in Chile:

> In the account of the cure of the blind man, the Gospel of the fourth Sunday of Lent shows the none too easy way which *leads to the discovery of this light*. In how many different ways the event narrated by the evangelist John is renewed in the life of human beings of every era!

> There are different ways, but the result is always the same: the light shines in the inner and outer darkness. The person sees. Even more: the person becomes a witness to the truth which comes from God ...
>
> Sister Teresa "de Los Andes", Teresa of Jesus, is the light of Christ for the whole Chilean Church: this Discalced Carmelite, the first fruits of holiness of the Teresian Camel of Latin America, today is enrolled among the saints of the universal Church.[232]

Spiritual Legacy of her writings

The life and writings of St Teresa of Los Andes were opened up to a wider English-speaking world with the publication of Fr Michael D. Griffin's translation of her letters in 1989, which went swiftly to further editions, followed closely by three other publications (see Bibliography).

Fr Michael Griffin concluded his introduction to the letters of St Teresa with this tribute:

> Through her beautiful letters, Saint Teresa of Jesus left a lasting imprint on the spirituality and theology of the Church. Through these letters she continues to speak to men and women today, inspiring all to draw nearer to God and to be filled with His abiding joy. The Saint's letters will convince readers that she herself was truly a modern miracle of nature and grace.
>
> She remains a special grace to the Church in our century. Her mission of love will continue forever because this young girl's life was perfectly consumed with and transformed by the fire of divine love. It is now evident that Saint Teresa of the Andes is destined to bring light and warmth and energy to the mission of the Church through the beauty of her holiness. And it is pleasing to know that she will be a continuing source of consolation to the world as it stands on the threshold of the third millennium of human history.[233]

The Legacy Of St Teresa Of Jesus Of Los Andes

I Wish I Could Set You Afire With That Love

Luis' Assessment

In Luis' testimony to his sister, he highlights an aspect of her life that endears her to ordinary people: within her ordinary life she achieved extraordinary things hidden from the world. The world praises external achievements: billions of money made, fame which is fame only because one is famous; awards, medals, prizes won, by which someone can measure their worth. Instead, in Juanita's life, it is the hidden things of the Spirit which are the most prized: her love, humility, generosity, fruits of the Spirit which are available to all who seek the Good, whether they are baptized or unbaptized:

> [I]t is astonishing – even objectively speaking, regardless of one's ideas or professed religious views – that a young girl like Juanita, one who died before the age of twenty, who left behind nothing concrete, nothing external, nothing valued by the world, should by the quality and power of her soul suddenly acquire universal homage and esteem.
>
> Is it possible for a life that was principally interior, in which there were no great events or adventures, to overcome the world?

The fact is that not everything great accomplished by humanity is revealed in external actions or events or tangible things. Often these works were the fruit of the Spirit, who, according to the mystics, is the secret inner fire that keeps the world alive.

The Spirit reaches the maximum dimensions in a saint. The saint is also the maximum victory of the invisible form from which the greatest human efficacy proceeds: one's ideas, dreams, one's mental stirrings. What is neither seen nor able to be touched is what profoundly moves the soul of the saint: how great the sweep of a saint's flight! A strange paradox in a time which proclaims the 'death of God' and in which, according to Marx, the forms of human work are the decisive factor in history.[234]

Pope St John Paul 11 echoed this thought about the ordinary life of Juanita in his Canonization homily:

As in the first reading which we heard from the Book of Samuel, Teresa does not stand out because of her 'appearance or lofty stature'. 'Not as man sees,' because man sees the appearance but the Lord 'looks into the heart'. (1 Samuel 16:7) Therefore, her short life of little more than 19 years, in her 11 months as a Carmelite, God made shine forth in her in an admirable way the light of His Son Jesus Christ, so that she could be a beacon and guide to a world which seems to be blind to the splendour of the divine.[235]

If we are thinking about her influence then we have to see how her influence has spread, especially in her own country of Chile and especially the young people there who see her as one of their own. Thousands of young people flood to her shrine every year to pray there. There is the witness of a love that burned within her, a joy that was infectious, springing from her love of God.

Juanita's Legacy

In thinking of Juanita's legacy, we have to ask first of all, why did God choose this particular young girl from her earliest years, guided her with extraordinary gifts throughout her life to the heights of holiness and why did she have to die at such an early age?

First, God saw in her one who would be consistently open to His guidance in the way of holiness. In the run-up to her reception of Holy Communion her young cousins and friends saw a marked change in her. She became more docile, less angry, less determined to have her own way. We can imagine what she might have become if she hadn't accepted God grace to guide her: there was her determination to 'win at all costs', and with her iron will she could have forced herself up in the secular world to places of eminence, but at a cost to others. She could have become very proud of her undoubted talents, her excellent intellect, her physical beauty, and used them to her own advantage. She could have become very self-centred and self-willed, and her character could have become hardened and cold, without thought of the needs of others.

I paint this portrait in order to stress that we all have a certain character, with its faults, but with gifts and talents, too, given by God which we can so easily use to our own self-aggrandisement instead of to His glory. The important thing is, how do we use all that we have and are? Do we use them for ourselves or for God? The choice is ours: 'I set before you life and death today: choose life!'

Juanita chose life, and at every stage in her life made that her choice, so that gradually, step by step, she was transformed, transfigured, into the image of Christ, allowing His life to flow strongly through her, increasingly unimpeded by sin, faults, resistance to God's grace. The divine paradox is, that, the more closely we are transformed into Christ, the more we become our true self, the self that God has willed for us, a unique individual with a unique place in His plan of salvation.

It is not by chance that three of our most recent saints, St Thérèse of Lisieux, St Elizabeth of the Trinity and St Teresa of Los Andes died young. This was in God's plan, so that the message He wished to give to the world should shine out with greater clarity. The shortness of their lives makes clear that their wisdom came from God. Their message could be made more accessible to ordinary people who wished to follow in their footsteps and be guided by their teaching, unimpeded by the varying circumstances of a long life.

In their youth is a message that the Gospel is always young, vibrant and creative. It will always find souls who will be drawn to its message of the divine attraction of Our Lord Jesus Christ. Our saints drew from the Scriptures, the sacraments and from the tradition of the Church all the nourishment they needed to grow in Christ and find in Him the peace, the joy, the holiness that only He can give, because He Himself is their peace, joy and holiness.

Appeal to Youth

Pope St John Paul 11 emphasized Juanita's appeal to young people because they could relate to her, a young person like themselves. She was popular, fond of sports, of swimming, horse-riding, playing tennis. But in his Canonization homily, he notes that with that initial appeal, Juanita leads them and challenges their lives in the secular world:

> She shouts it out particularly to the young people who hunger for the truth and seek a light which will give direction to their lives. To young people who are being allured by the continuous messages and stimuli of an erotic culture, a society which mistakes the hedonistic exploitation of another for genuine love, which is self-giving, this young virgin of the Andes today proclaims the beauty and happiness that comes from a pure heart.[236]

The secular world has become enslaved to an erotic culture and hedonistic exploitation to an alarming degree, even more so than in Juanita's time. In her search for purity of heart she met with teasing from her cousins and pupils, but with a charming graciousness continued to be herself. To ignore teasing when she was only a young child shows strength of character. Later, when she was disinclined to take part in flamboyant dances or wear low-cut dresses, she managed, unobtrusively, to play for the dancing instead, and only wear modest dresses which at the same time didn't make her look the odd one out.

When girls, especially, are expected to wear very revealing clothes, but feel, deep down, that it doesn't express who they really are, Juanita's example and prayer for them could give them the courage to be themselves.

Of course, purity, chastity, is not a negative message as it is often portrayed. 'Blessed are the pure in heart, for they shall see God'. The message of purity has strength, beauty and attractiveness because it gives courage, delight in the good, and the superlative promise given by Jesus Christ Himself that the pure in heart will see God, not simply in the fulness of vision in heaven but heaven also here on earth, when it becomes, as St Elizabeth of the Trinity said, 'heaven begun and always in progress'.

The Perfect Role Model

Young people look for a role model who will help them make sense of their world, someone they can look up to, admire and emulate. So often this will be a pop star, a film star, a sports personality. For Juanita, her only role model was Jesus Christ. Her other model was Mary, the perfect example of one who gave the perfect human response to God. Meditating on Jesus' birth at Bethlehem and Mary's contemplation of Him, she wrote:

> She sees that little Child, crying in the arms of His poor Mother, and those tears are the ones of the One who is infinite Joy. How can we fail to love that Jesus with our whole soul? He, who is uncreated Beauty, He, Wisdom eternal, He, Goodness, Life and Love. how can our soul

fail to be inflamed with charity at the sight of that God dragged through the streets of Jerusalem with His cross on His shoulders; at the sight of that God becoming food for His creatures, transforming Himself in bread in order to be one with them, to divinize and convert them into Himself? Oh, love Jesus. Who can ever return your love better? He thirsts for your heart. Don't you feel that when after receiving Communion He says to you: 'Daughter, give me your heart'? [237]

The Darkness of Sin

From a very early age Juanita became aware of sin and did her best to live far away from it. On 8 December 1915 she made her first vow of chastity, which she renewed yearly until making her Carmelite vows on her deathbed. The sins committed against the body are, in a very true way, more serious than others because they damage the person from within and fight against the dignity of the person. Chastity is almost a concept for mockery today, but Juanita made every effort to maintain her dignity as a Christian whose 'body is not your own', as St Paul said (1 Corinthians 6:19); God owns it and we have to preserve it pure for Him.

Because of her striving for purity Juanita was acutely aware of the least fault that sullied it. In her visions of the crucified and tortured Jesus, He made her aware of the full horror of sin, and as a pure victim she united herself with Him, taking upon herself, with Jesus, the pain of sin.

Her example is a call for the world to take sin seriously. It is an almost alien concept now in the secular world where almost everything is permissible. In her visions of Christ she learnt to a deep degree the damage that sin does, not only to the person, but that it is, above all, sin against God Himself and His design and plan for the human person. That is why she learnt to treat herself and others with the utmost dignity as children of God, made in His image, and was encouraged to pass through outward appearances to see Christ in the other.

Living the Christian Life

At her baptism, Juanita was immersed into the death and resurrection of Jesus, given new life in Him and made a member of His Church. The Blessed Trinity took up His abode in her. Our Lady became her heavenly Mother guiding her ever step. She received and met her Lord in the Eucharist, immersing herself in the blazing love of the Sacred Heart and the Sacred Humanity of Jesus. By way of the Cross, she was led into to the inner life of the Most Blessed Trinity, which had always been dwelling within her and was gradually revealed to her.

This is a description of Juanita's spiritual life, and it is the way of life open to every Christian by reason of their baptism. Her example calls us, invites us, urges us, to follow in her steps, for it is the way of the Gospel.

Perhaps the Scriptures have become so familiar to us that we tend to overlook the radical nature of the call of Jesus and what he expects of His followers. He tells us that if we prefer father or mother to Him we are not worthy of Him. He tells us that if our hand offends, then cut it off. He says that if we insult another it is as good as murder. He tells us to take up our cross daily to follow Him. All these examples have the hyperbole of the middle eastern way of speaking, but this emphasises the radical nature of the Christian life.

Juanita took the call of Jesus seriously; with the help of His grace she did her best to rid her life of everything that was not pleasing to Him, refining all the traits of her character so that they were at His service rather than at her own.

Perhaps the reason why she attained holiness so quickly was that her life was free of extraneous elements; in her life everything that is required for holiness was laid bare and evident. She was serious about becoming holy and this took first place in her heart.

Each person will have a different and unique relationship with God, and it is only by being open to Him and His grace, committed to doing His will and by embracing the cross, His love will come to fruition in us.

For those whose vocation it is to live in the world and yet stay close to God, Teresa composed a beautiful little prayer:

> I keep myself closely united to Our Lord within the home of my soul; so, that has to be my little cell for now. Whenever I go out on the street or to the theatre or take a walk, I tell Our Lord: 'My Jesus, although perhaps no one here is thinking about You, but here's a heart that belongs completely to You. I adore you, I love You. Make me Yours always'. In this way I keep myself recollected and removed from worldly things.[238]

To those who are looking for peace in their lives, however difficult their lives may be, Teresa points the way to where peace is found:

> I don't know how to repay Our Lord for so much love, so much kindness to a creature who deserves to be utterly forgotten. I find myself immersed in such a tremendous atmosphere of peace and love … and at the same time, it seems as though I'm in eternity already, in that land beyond change. These are the feelings evoked in my soul by a union with God.[239]

What use is the contemplative life?

Many question the usefulness of the contemplative life and cannot understand it. If someone was truly concerned for the salvation of souls, goes the argument, then surely they would serve them in a concrete way, in teaching, nursing, serving the poor, for example, showing the fruits of their prayer in action. These are perfectly valid vocations, as the many active orders attest; many lay people, too, are drawn to this way of life. But there is room and legitimacy for the purely contemplative life. Of course, a deep prayer life can go hand in hand with an active apostolate, and every vocation, be it in the married state, work in the world, an active religious vocation, is a call to holiness. Equally, some called to the contemplative life are not all called to high states of contemplative prayer. What Juanita underlines is that prayer is essential in every walk of life, and the closer we come to Our Lord the more fruitful our apostolate will be and our influence over souls. As Jesus Himself said: 'Without Me you can do nothing'. (John 15:5) This is the witness of the contemplative life:

> One who is united and identified with Jesus, can do all things. And it seems to me that only through prayer can this be achieved. Although others may say that souls are saved through the apostolate and through prayer, I see it as much more difficult, for this requires a great union with the Redeemer, for to save souls is nothing but to give them to Jesus and one who does not have Jesus can give nothing. Normally those in the active life find it much more difficult to become completely one with God, since outward things and one's dealings with the world distract and separate them from Jesus. Besides, it seems to me that self-love can become involved when we experience success, a danger Carmelites don't have, for they never know how many souls they save by prayer and sacrifice, and perhaps from her Carmelite cell, she conquers, as do missionaries, millions of nonbelievers scattered to the ends of the earth.[240]

Most are not called to the cloister but are called to live a life of Christian witness in the world. While at school, Juanita demonstrated how we should live that life, not seeing created things as without worth, but seeing them in the light of Christ. She would do her best at school, because she recognized the gifts she had been given, and wanted to use them to the best of her ability, and to give glory to God. It is in this context that we should read the letter she sent to Luis shortly after her entry into Carmel. By looking to Christ, by putting Him first, everything else takes its proper place:

Please, dear Luis, let me speak to you, heart to heart. Your Carmelite sister comes to show you what is the motive of our life, what is the prime goal of every person, of every Christian: 'To know, to love and to serve God here on earth to gain heaven'. What does everything on earth, science, glory, honours, matter, Luis dear, if all of them come to an end? Death does away with everything. Only a single knowledge, only one truth will not be taken away, because it is based on what is immutable. Only one good, one love can never be destroyed, because it's eternal and infinite. Everything passes away in life but our good deeds. We too will pass away, Luis. Only one Being will remain always the same: God. Let's love Him, even before knowing Him. God alone is worthy of being known, because He is infinite. Dear Luis, why not seek that Being, the only necessary One? Let's love Him and we'll be happy, because God is the object of our understanding and will.[241]

The Eucharist and Our Lady

St John Bosco had a dream in which he saw a boat, representing the Church, buffeted on all sides and nearly sinking. But then it sailed between two pillars, representing the Eucharist and Our Lady, and all was calm and safe. The message was that as long as the Church remained true to the Eucharist and Our Lady, she would remain calm and at peace.

The same could be said of Juanita. All her life she remained faithful and true to her devotion to the Blessed Sacrament, finding her nourishment in receiving Holy Communion daily when at all possible and making a spiritual communion when she could not. She could, with truth, be called an apostle of the Eucharist, calling people to celebrate the Mass with the consecrated priest, sharing in the priesthood of Christ. She calls us to ponder the depths of the Eucharist, living every day in union with the Eucharistic Christ, spending time with Him before the Blessed Sacrament. As she wrote to Amelia Martinez,

Receive Communion as well [as going to Mass] and be deeply aware of the One who visits you, infinite love, divine madness; of One who not only became man like ourselves, but who became bread. After you receive Communion, ask Jesus, the God you hold prisoner in your soul, to stay with you throughout the day so that you may love Him and give Him thanks.[242]

Before she left for Carmel, Juanita gave to Luis the precious statue of Our Lady, which had been her constant companion as she explained to him:

Luis, before I go, I want to leave you my statue of the Most Holy Virgin as a sign of our perpetual union. It has been my constant companion. She has been my intimate confidante from the most tender years of my life. She has listened to me tell of my joys and sorrows. She has often comforted my heart broken with sorrow. Luis, dear, I'm leaving the statue with you to take my place. Talk to her, heart-to-heart, just as you do to me. When you feel lonely, as I often do, look at her and you'll see her smiling face, telling you: 'Your Mother won't ever leave you alone'.[243]

Prayer

Prayer was indispensable to Juanita as it is to every Christian, because by it we come to know Christ Jesus and live in union with Him. She received many exceptional graces that are not given to everyone, but by what was given to her we come to recognise what is given to everyone:

If you give yourself to prayer, you'll find that God will show Himself to you, and make you fall in love with Him. In prayer our soul seeks Him out, and if we do so, wanting to know and love Him, Jesus will raise a bit the veil that conceals Him and show us His divine Face, radiant with beauty and sweetness. There are times when He will open His Heart's wound, and will show us the treasures of His infinite goodness and love. At other times He lets His sweet voice be heard, leaving the soul consumed by love and repentance.[244]

Love

Juanita was in love with God and couldn't understand how anyone couldn't love One so beautiful and so full of love. She calls everyone, through prayer, through seeing God in all things everywhere, to love Him as 'madly' as she does, because it is simply returning love to Him who first loves us:

> Let's love eternal Love, infinite and immutable Love. let's love God madly, for He loved us in His eternity. Without needing us, His whole powerful work was done for humanity. He placed everything at our disposal. He continually sustains and nourishes us. And in order not to be separated from us in eternity, He gave us His only begotten Son. God became a creature. He suffered and died for us. God made Himself nourishment for His creatures. Have you ever thought deeply about the infinite madness of this love? Believe me, I feel my soul overwhelmed with gratitude and love. My life is spent contemplating that incomprehensible Goodness, and my soul suffers when I see that Love is unknown. I plunge myself deeply into His grandeur, into His wisdom. But when I think about His goodness, my heart is speechless. I adore Him.[245]

The Infinite God

Juanita became speechless before the infinite God. Her God and the God whom Christians adore and profess is no narrow God, as He is so often portrayed. Rather, as Juanita illustrates, union with God of infinite love expands the heart, increases love, not only for God Himself but for all the dear humanity for whom Jesus offered His life. Juanita felt that her search for true happiness could be satisfied only by God, who is with her at every step of her journey. All lesser things failed to satisfy. She wrote this letter after hearing of the death of her Uncle Andrew:

> What an immense difference there is between the death of one who is Christian and one who is not. The latter finds nothing but the emptiness, the nothingness, the coldness of the tomb. A Christian finds the goal of his exile, of his sufferings, the beginning of his eternal joys. A Christian finds, in short, his God, who is his Father, who has been watching over him at every step of his journey through goodness and sorrow. There is His Father, His arms stretched out to receive him and give him his crown.[246]

This is balanced by her conviction that it was her duty to use her gifts of intelligence, joy and compassion to their utmost. It gave to her character a spaciousness, an openness to all that is good in the world, while at the same time spending her time in ardent intercession, in an agony of prayer at the sin that distorted it. In the West, especially, the atheistic and secular agenda paints Christianity and God as being narrow, constricting and against life. Juanita shows us the beauty of the Christian Faith, how it expands the soul, when a person sets out on the road to God, guided by His grace. As Jesus gently but firmly guided Juanita, showing her her faults, she became increasingly free, because it is our sins, failings and faults that weigh us down and prevent us to receive the genuine happiness and joy that only God can give, as she wrote to her sister Lucia:

> I want to tell you about my happiness. Yes, I want you to feel for just a moment, the happiness of belonging entirely to God, but there's no human language that can express the divine feelings in which my soul finds itself submerged. I've given Him everything, it's true, but I've also come to possess the One who is Everything.[247]

And to her sister, Rebecca, who would indeed answer her sister's prayer and follow her to Carmel:

> Let's live loving Love, my little sister. Let's be hosts of praise to the Most Holy Trinity. And how? By fulfilling God's will at every moment. If you could but know the happiness that floods my soul at every moment of my life hidden in God! I would rather not know or deal with anything but Him.[248]

Juanita's Wish for us

As has been often stressed, her dominant characteristic was joy, happiness, enjoyment of the good things that God gives, sharing generously with others of her time, her wisdom and her friendship. She longed that they share in her joy at being loved by God and realising that He has that particular love for each one of them – and for us. As she herself said, 'I wish I could get you to know and love God and love God the way I do:

> Oh, if you could see just for a moment how my Jesus loves me! It's as if there were no other creature in the world He loves, since His love is shown me in the smallest details. How I would want you to love Him! Who could open your soul's eyes that you might see His captivating and infinite beauty that you might understand the ecstasy of His infinite love.[249]

As always, she pointed her friends, her family, everyone, to where true peace and joy are to be found, in Jesus Christ:

> Look at Him with the eyes of your soul. Contemplate His beauty. Go into His Heart; it is full of love for you. Think of how much He suffered that you might have heaven, and God for all eternity. I think of Jesus often in the Eucharist. He longs to be with you, for He loves you with a special love, since He chose you that He might live in unity with you.[250]

> How I wish, that from the time I had the use of reason, I had dedicated myself to knowing this God who's so good, this Being who's infinitely beautiful, the only One worthy of being known. Love Him, because He's the only One worthy of our love. live in Him more than in yourself. God is closer to us than we are to ourselves. God fills us, completely permeates us, because He's immense and everything exists in Him. God in His greatness never forgets His creatures and is constantly working with love and paternal solicitude ... give yourself to Him, love Him and follow Him.[251]

1 **Introduction**
D.Griffin, O.C.D., (Comp.), *Testimonies to Saint Teresa of the Andes*, (Hubertus, WI, Teresian Charism Press 1991), p. 13.

2 Michael D.Griffin, O.C.D., (Comp.), *A New Hymn to God*, (Hubertus, WI, Teresian Charism Press 1993), p. 2.

3 *Ibid.*, p.14.

Chapter One, Born in the Midst of Riches

4 Michael D.Griffin, O.C.D., (Comp.), *Testimonies to Saint Teresa of the Andes*, (Hubertus, WI, Teresian Charism Press 1991), p. 80.

5 Michael D. Griffin, O'C.D, *God, the Joy of My Life: a Biography of Saint Teresa of Jesus of the Andes,* (Hubertus, WI, Teresian Charism Press 1995), p. 184.

6 *Ibid.*, p. 188.

7 *Ibid.*, p. 190.

8 *Testimonies*, p. 59

9 Michael D.Griffin, O.C.D., (trans.) *Letters of Saint Teresa of Jesus of the Andes*, (Hubertus, WI, Teresian Charism Press 1994), L. 87.

10 *God, the Joy of My Life*, p. 197.

Chapter Two, My Family, Those Beings I Love so Much

11 Michael D.Griffin, O.C.D., (trans.) *Letters of Saint Teresa of Jesus of the Andes*, (Hubertus, WI, Teresian Charism Press 1994), L. 21.

12 Michael D.Griffin, O.C.D., (Comp.), *Testimonies to Saint Teresa of the Andes*, (Hubertus, WI, Teresian Charism Press 1991), p. 72ff.

13 *Ibid.*, p.76.

14 *Ibid.*, p. 89ff.

15 *Ibid.* p.62.

16 *Ibid.*, p.63.

17 Michael D. Griffin, O'C.D, *God, the Joy of My Life: a Biography of Saint Teresa of Jesus of the Andes,* (Hubertus, WI, Teresian Charism Press 1995), p.199.

18 **Chapter Three, That Terrible Return to School**
Michael D. Griffin, O.C.D., (Comp.), *Testimonies to Saint Teresa of the Andes*, (Hubertus, WI, Teresian Charism Press 1991), p. 67ff.

19 *Ibid.*, p.67.

20 Michael D. Griffin, O.C.D., (trans.) *Letters of Saint Teresa of Jesus of the Andes*, (Hubertus, WI, Teresian Charism Press 1994), L.13.

21 Michael D. Griffin, O'C.D, *God, the Joy of My Life: a Biography of Saint Teresa of Jesus of the Andes,* (Hubertus, WI, Teresian Charism Press 1995), p.200.

22 *God, the Joy of My Life*, p. 181.

Chapter Four, The Amazon

23 Michael D. Griffin, O.C.D., (trans.) *Letters of Saint Teresa of Jesus of the Andes*, (Hubertus, WI, Teresian Charism Press 1994), L. 4.

24 *Ibid.*, L. 5.

25 Michael D. Griffin, O.C.D., (Comp.), *Testimonies to Saint Teresa of the Andes*, (Hubertus,

WI, Teresian Charism Press 1991), p.81ff.

26 *Letters,* L. 8.

27 *Ibid.,* L. 10.

28 *Ibid.*

29 Michael D. Griffin, O'C.D, *God, the Joy of My Life: a Biography of Saint Teresa of Jesus of the Andes,* (Hubertus, WI, Teresian Charism Press 1995), p. 221.

30 *Ibid.,,* p. 230.

Chapter Five, Mater Amabilis

31 Michael D. Griffin, O'C.D, *God, the Joy of My Life: a Biography of Saint Teresa of Jesus of the Andes,* (Hubertus, WI, Teresian Charism Press 1995), p. 230.

32 *Ibid.,* p. 233.

33 *Ibid.,* p. 261.

34 *Ibid.,* p. 226.

35 *Ibid.,* p. 229ff.

36 *Ibid,* p. 244ff.

37 *Ibid.* p. 261.

38 *Ibid.* p. 234.

39 *Ibid.* p. 246.

40 Michael D. Griffin, O.C.D., (trans.) *Letters of Saint Teresa of Jesus of the Andes,* (Hubertus, WI, Teresian Charism Press 1994), L.14.

41 *Ibid.*

42 *Ibid.,* L. 15.

43 *God, the Joy of My Life,* p .249.

44 *Letters 17*

45 *Ibid.*

Chapter Six, Dear Old Algorrobo

46 Michael D. Griffin, O.C.D., (trans.) *Letters of Saint Teresa of Jesus of the Andes,* (Hubertus, WI, Teresian Charism Press 1994), L. 19.

47 *Ibid.,* p. 21.

48 *Ibid.,* L. 19.

49 Michael D. Griffin, O.C.D., (Comp.), *Testimonies to Saint Teresa of the Andes,* (Hubertus, WI, Teresian Charism Press 1991), p.81.

50 St Elizabeth of the Trinity: *Complete Works, Volume 2,* (Washington DC, ICS Publications. 1995), Letter 90.

51 *Letters,* L. 20.

52 *Ibid.,* L. 25.

53 Michael D. Griffin, O'C.D, *God, the Joy of My Life: a Biography of Saint Teresa of Jesus of the Andes,* (Hubertus, WI, Teresian Charism Press 1995), p.207.

54 *Letters,* L. 24.

55 *Testimonies,* p. 80.

56 *Letters,* L.23

57   *Letters*, L. 23

58   *Testimonies*, p.80

59   *Letters* L. 21.

60   *ibid*, L. 20.

Chapter Seven, Farewell to School

61   Michael D. Griffin, O'C.D, *God, the Joy of My Life: a Biography of Saint Teresa of Jesus of the Andes,* (Hubertus, WI, Teresian Charism Press 1995), p. 264.

62   *Ibid.,* p. 265.

63   *Ibid.*

64   *Ibid.,* p. 267.

65   *Ibid.,* p. 268.

66   *Cf.* L 31.

67   *God, the Joy of My Life,* p. 274.

Chapter Eight, I'm Famous for my Fits of Laughter

68   Michael D. Griffin, O'C.D, *God, the Joy of My Life: a Biography of Saint Teresa of Jesus of the Andes,* (Hubertus, WI, Teresian Charism Press 1995), p. 278.

69   Michael D. Griffin, O.C.D., (trans.) *Letters of Saint Teresa of Jesus of the Andes,* (Hubertus, WI, Teresian Charism Press 1994), L. 45.

70   *Letters,* L. 36.

71   *Ibid.,* L. 37.

72   *Ibid.,* L. 36.

73   *Ibid.,* L. 41.

74   *Ibid.,* L. 42.

75   *Ibid.,* L. 44.

76   *Ibid.* L 43.

77   **Chapter Nine, That Dovecote Nest**
Cf. Michael D. Griffin, O'C.D, *God, the Joy of My Life: a Biography of Saint Teresa of Jesus of the Andes,* (Hubertus, WI, Teresian Charism Press 1995), p. 280.

78   Michael D. Griffin, O.C.D., (trans.) *Letters of Saint Teresa of Jesus of the Andes,* (Hubertus, WI, Teresian Charism Press 1994), *40* L. 51.

79   *Ibid.*

80   *God, the Joy of My Life,* p. 285.35

81   *Letters* L. 52.

82   *Ibid.,* L. 67.

83   *Ibid.,* L .54.

84   *Ibid.,* L.70.

85   *Ibid.,* L.73.

86   *Ibid.,* L. 78.

87   **Chapter Ten, The Horizons are Infinite**
Michael D. Griffin, O.C.D., (trans.) *Letters of Saint Teresa of Jesus of the Andes,* (Hubertus, WI, Teresian Charism Press 1994), L. 81.

88   *Ibid.*, L. 93.

Chapter Eleven, I'm Happy

89   Michael D. Griffin, O.C.D., (trans.) *Letters of Saint Teresa of Jesus of the Andes*, (Hubertus, WI, Teresian Charism Press 1994), L.136.

90   Michael D. Griffin, O'C.D, *God, the Joy of My Life: a Biography of Saint Teresa of Jesus of the Andes*, (Hubertus, WI, Teresian Charism Press 1995), p. 283.

91   *Letters*, L. 98.

92   *Ibid.*

93   *God, the Joy of My Life*, p.298.

94   *Ibid*, p.300ff.

95   *Letters*, L.96.

96   *Ibid.*, L. 98.

97   *Ibid.*, L. 198.

98   *Ibid.* L. 103.

99   *Ibid.*, L. 108.

100   *Ibid.*

101   *Ibid.* L. 100.

102   *Ibid.*, L. 101.

103   *Ibid.*, L.108.

104   *Ibid.*, L. 138.

105   *Ibid.*, L.127.

106   *Ibid.*, L. 129.

107   *Ibid.*, L. 148.

108   *Ibid.*, L 62.

109   *Ibid*, L. 164.

110   Michael D. Griffin, O.C.D., (Comp.), *Testimonies to Saint Teresa of the Andes*, (Hubertus, WI, Teresian Charism Press 1991), p.55.

PART TWO, Jesus, my Ideal, my infinite Ideal
Introduction
Chapter One, Caught in the Nets of the Divine Fisherman

111   Michael D. Griffin, O'C.D, *God, the Joy of My Life: a Biography of Saint Teresa of Jesus of the Andes*, (Hubertus, WI, Teresian Charism Press 1995), p.39ff.

112   St John of the Cross, (Collected Works, Washington DC, ICS Publications 1973), *The Ascent of Mount Carmel* Ch. 22:5. p. 180.

113   Michael D. Griffin, O.C.D., (trans.) *Letters of Saint Teresa of Jesus of the Andes*, (Hubertus, WI, Teresian Charism Press 1994), L. 138.

114   *Ibid.*, l. 136.

115   *Ibid.* L. 133.

116   Christopher O'Mahoney, Ed. *St Thérèse of Lisieux by Those Who Knew Her* (Dublin, Veritas Publcations,1975), p. 261.

117   St Elizabeth of the Trinity: *Complete Works, Volume 2,* (Washington DC, ICS Publications, 1995), Letter 122.

118   Michael D. Griffin, O.C.D., (trans.) *Letters of Saint Teresa of Jesus of the Andes,* (Hubertus, WI, Teresian Charism Press 1994), L. 40.

119   *Ibid.*

120   *Ibid.,* L. 8.

121   *Ibid.,* L. 110.,

122   *Ibid.,* L. 105.

123   *Ibid.,* L.121.

124   *Ibid.,* L. 37.

125   *Ibid.,* L. 12.

Chapter Two, The goal of prayer is to kindle in us the love of our God

126   Michael D. Griffin, O.C.D., (trans.) *Letters of Saint Teresa of Jesus of the Andes,* (Hubertus, WI, Teresian Charism Press 1994), L. 82..

127   St Teresa of Avila, Collected Works, Vol 2, *Interior Castle* (Kavanaugh & Rodriguez (trans.), Washington DC ICS Publications, 1980), V1:7:6, p. 399.

128   *Letters.,* L. 52.

129   *Ibid.,* L. 121.

130   *Ibid.,* L. 109.

131   Michael D. Griffin, O'C.D, *God, the Joy of My Life: a Biography of Saint Teresa of Jesus of the Andes,* (Hubertus, WI, Teresian Charism Press 1989), p. 292.

132   *Ibid.,* p.224.

133   St John of the Cross, (Collected Works, Washington DC, ICS Publications 1973), *The Ascent of Mount Carmel* Bk 11, Ch. 15: 5).

134   *Letters,* L. 78.

135   *Ascent* Bk 11 Ch 13:1

136   *Ibid.,* Ch. 13:7.

137   *God, the Joy of My Life,* p. 304.

138   *Ibid.,* p. 254.

139   *Letters,* L. 27.

140   *God, the Joy of My Life,* p.190.

141   *Letters,* L. 87

142   *God, the Joy of My Life,* p. 192.

143   *Letters,* p. 87.

144   *Ascent,* 11: 29:1

145   *Letters,* L.66.

146   *Letters* L. 138.

147   *Ascent,* 11:31:1.

148   *God, the Joy of My Life,* p.201.

149   *Letters,* L. 29.

150   *Ibid.,* L.36.

Chapter Three, Jesus is my Nourishment.

151   Michael D. Griffin, O.C.D., (trans.) *Letters of Saint Teresa of Jesus of the Andes,* (Hubertus, WI, Teresian Charism Press 1994), L.87.

152   *Letters,* L. 141.

153   Michael D. Griffin, O'C.D, *God, the Joy of My Life: a Biography of Saint Teresa of Jesus of the Andes,* (Hubertus, WI, Teresian Charism Press 1989), p. 199.

154   Fr Michael Müller, C.S.S.R. *The Blessed Eucharist* (Rockford, Tan Publications), p. 2.

155   *Letters,* L. 117.

156   *Ibid.* L. 151.

157   *Ibid.* L. 114.

158   *Ibid.,* L. 128.

159   *Ibid.* L. 74.

160   *Ibid.* L. 29.

161   *Ibid.,* L. 30.

162   *Ibid.,* L. 56.

163   Michael D. Griffin, O.C.D., (Comp.), *Testimonies to Saint Teresa of the Andes,* (Hubertus, WI, Teresian Charism Press 1991), p.194ff.

164   *Letters,* L. 83.

165   *Ibid.,* L. 122.

166   *God, the Joy of My Life,* p. 273.

167   St Elizabeth of the Trinity: *Complete Works, Volume 2,* (Washington DC, ICS Publications, 1995), Letter 91.

168   *Letters,* L. 130.

169   *Ibid.,* L. 114.

170   *Ibid.* L. 109.

171   *God, the Joy of My Life,* p. 301.

172   *Letters,* L. 145.

173   *Ibid.* L. 133.

174   *Ibid.,* L.116.

175   *Ibid.,* L. 141.

176   *Ibid.,* L. 114.

177   *Ibid.,* L. 116.

178   *God, the Joy of My Life,* p.222.

Chapter Four, I Really Love the Most Holy Virgin

179   Michael D. Griffin, O.C.D., (trans.) *Letters of Saint Teresa of Jesus of the Andes,* (Hubertus, WI, Teresian Charism Press 1994), L. 73.

180   Michael D. Griffin, O'C.D, *God, the Joy of My Life: a Biography of Saint Teresa of Jesus of the Andes,* (Hubertus, WI, Teresian Charism Press 1989), p. 221ff.

181   *Ibid.,* p.208ff.

182   *Letters*, L.40.

Chapter Five, What does Suffering Matter if a person loves?

183   Michael D. Griffin, O'C.D, *God, the Joy of My Life: a Biography of Saint Teresa of Jesus of the Andes*, (Hubertus, WI, Teresian Charism Press 1989), p. 207ff.

184   Michael D. Griffin, O.C.D., (trans.) *Letters of Saint Teresa of Jesus of the Andes*, (Hubertus, WI, Teresian Charism Press 1994), L.15.

185   St Elizabeth of the Trinity: *Complete Works, Volume 2,* (Washington DC, ICS Publications, 1995), L.169.

186   *God, the Joy of My Life*, p.207.

187   *Ibid.* p.220.

188   *Ibid.*, p. 236.

189   *Ibid.*, p. 199.

190   *Ibid.*, p. 275.,

191   *Letters*, L. 16.

192   St Teresa of Avila, Collected Works, Vol 2, *The Way of Perfection*,(Kavanaugh & Rodriguez (trans.), Washington DC ICS Publications, 1980). Ch 18:2, p. 102

193   *God, the Joy of My Life*, p.253.

194   *Ibid.*, p. 252.

195   *Ibid.*, p. 203.

196   *Ibid.*, p. 254ff.

197   *Ibid.*, p. 260ff.80

198   *Letters*, L. 29.

199   *God, the Joy of My Life*, p.260.

200   Dijon Carmel, *Elizabeth de la Trinité, Souvenirs*, (Paris, Editions St-Paul,[1946]) p. 71ff.

201   *God, the Joy of My Life*, p. 228.

Chapter Six, This darkness is followed by a bit of light

202   Michael D. Griffin, O'C.D, *God, the Joy of My Life: a Biography of Saint Teresa of Jesus of the Andes*, (Hubertus, WI, Teresian Charism Press 1989), p. 299.

203   Michael D. Griffin, O.C.D., (trans.) *Letters of Saint Teresa of Jesus of the Andes*, (Hubertus, WI, Teresian Charism Press 1994), L. 145.

204   John Clarke, (trans),*Story of a Soul, the Autobiography of St Thérèse of Lisieux*, (Washington DC, ICS Publications,3rd Edition1996), p.211ff.

205   Michael D. Griffin, O'C.D, *God, the Joy of My Life: a Biography of Saint Teresa of Jesus of the Andes*, (Hubertus, WI, Teresian Charism Press 1989), p.302ff.

206   *Ibid.*, p. 306.

207   *Ibid.*, p.304ff.

208   *Ibid.*, p. 305ff.

209   *Ibid.*, p. 306.

210   *Letters*, L. 141.

211   St Teresa of Avila, Collected Works, Vol 2, *Interior Castle* (Kavanaugh & Rodriguez (trans.), Washington DC ICS Publications, 1980). Interior Castle Ch 9: 4, p.411ff.

212   *Letters*, L. 67.

213   Michael D. Griffin, O'C.D, *God, the Joy of My Life: a Biography of Saint Teresa of Jesus of the Andes*, (Hubertus, WI, Teresian Charism Press 1989), p.294.

214   *Interior Castle* – Introduction, p. 275.

215   *God, the Joy of My Life*, p. 304.

Chapter Seven, The Perfection of love

216   *Interior Castle* V11:2, p. 433.

217   Michael D. Griffin, O.C.D., (trans.) *Letters of Saint Teresa of Jesus of the Andes*, (Hubertus, WI, Teresian Charism Press 1994), L. 66.

218   *Ibid*, L. 105.

219   *Interior Castle* V11:1:6, p. 430.

220   *Letters*, L. 122

221   *Letters*, L.121.

222   Michael D. Griffin, O.C.D., (Comp.), *Testimonies to Saint Teresa of the Andes*, (Hubertus, WI, Teresian Charism Press 1991), p.47.

223   *Letters*, L.121.

PART THREE, AFTERWARD, Live in love, live in heaven, live in God

224   Michael D. Griffin, O'C.D, *God, the Joy of My Life: a Biography of Saint Teresa of Jesus of the Andes*, (Hubertus, WI, Teresian Charism Press 1989), p.159.

225   *Letters*, L.160.

226   *Ibid.*, p.148.

227   *God, the Joy of My Life*, p.77

228   *Letters*, L.159.

229   *Testimonies*, p. 203.

230   *God, the Joy of My Life*, p.96ff.

231   *Ibid.* p. 320ff.

232   Michael D. Griffin, O.D.C., (Comp)., *A New Hymn to God*, (Washington DC, Teresian Charism Press, 1993), p. 11ff.

233   *Letters*, p. XXV111.

The Legacy of St Teresa of Jesus of Los Andes, I wish I could set you afire with that love

234   Michael D. Griffin, O.C.D., (Comp.), *Testimonies to Saint Teresa of the Andes*, (Hubertus, WI, Teresian Charism Press 1991), 91ff.

235   *Testimonies*, p. 13.

236   Michael D. Griffin, O.D.C., (Comp)., *A New Hymn to God*, (Washington DC, Teresian Charism Press, 1993),p. 14.99

237   Michael D. Griffin, O.C.D., (trans.) *Letters of Saint Teresa of Jesus of the Andes*, (Hubertus, WI, Teresian Charism Press 1994), L.136.

238   *Letters* L. 36.

239   *Ibid.* L. 97.

240   *Ibid.* L. 130.

241 *Ibid.*, L. 96.
242 *Ibid.*, L. 141.
243 *Ibid.* L. 81.
244 *Ibid.*, L 121.
245 *Ibid.*
246 *Ibid.*, L. 126.
247 *Ibid.*, L.112.
248 *Ibid.*, L. 114.
249 *Ibid.*, L. 121.
250 *Ibid.*, L.142.
251 *Ibid.*, L 108.

BIBLIOGRAPHY

John Clarke, O.C.D., (Trans.), *Story of a Soul, The Autobiography of St Thérèse of Lisieux,* Washington DC, ICs Publications, 1996.

Michael D. Griffin O.C.D., (Comp.), *A New Hymn to God,* Hubertus, WI, Teresian Charism Press, 1993.

Michael D. Griffin O.C.D.*God the Joy of My Life: A Biography of Saint Teresa of Jesus of the Andes.* Hubertus, WI: Teresian Charism Press. 1995.

Michael D. Griffin O.C.D. (Trans.), *Letters of Saint Teresa of Jesus of the Andes,* Hubertus, WI: Teresian Charism Press. 1994.

Michael D. Griffin O.C.D. (Comp.), *Testimonies to Saint Teresa of the Andes,* Hubertus, WI: Teresian Charism Press. 1991.

Kieran Kavanaugh., O.C.D., and Otilio Rodriguez, O.C.D., (Trans), *The Collected Works of St John of the Cross,* Washington DC, ICS Publications, 1973.

Kieran Kavanaugh., O.C.D., and Otilio Rodriguez, O.C.D., (Trans), *The Collected Works of St Teresa of Avila,* Washington DC, ICS Publications, 1985.

Anne Englund Nash (Trans.), *The Complete Works of Elizabeth of the Trinity,* Volume 2, Washington DC., ICS Publications, 1995.

Scripture quotations are from the Revised Standard Version, Catholic Edition, with permission

Further reading:

Jennifer Moorcroft, *God is All Joy, the Life of Saint Teresa of Los Andes,* Los Angeles, CA, Westwood Books Publishing, 2021.

www.ingramcontent.com/pod-product-compliance
Lightning Source LLC
Chambersburg PA
CBHW071432070526
44578CB00001B/79